PRAISE FOR *MORE CHRIST, MORE ME*

"Eunice took me on a journey through her life that at first, while interesting, I thought had nothing to do with my life experience as a Latino man. As I reached the heart of the book, I realized she was speaking directly to emotional dynamics I've also been dealing with in my family of origin. Her struggles and triumphs empowered me to find freedom in my own life. This book sheds light on an issue many probably deal with unconsciously and paves the road to find the strength to confront it."

—ALEXANDER MORA, Founder and Executive Director of Love Story Foundation

"This is the book I wish I'd had when I was younger and feeling lost in my identity formation. It would've given me empowering and clarifying language, helped me process and reframe some of my experiences, and most of all, validated and comforted me to know I was not alone and there was nothing inherently wrong with me and the struggles I was having. It was healing to read Eunice's narrative because it reflects my own faith journey, as well as the ways I eventually learned to integrate my views and feelings on faith, family, ethnic identity, and the many conflicting expectations and values of being a child of immigrants. I recommend this book for anyone who is struggling to navigate their own views on God, the world, and themselves."

—HANNAH LEE, Oak and Stone Marriage and Family Therapy Center

"Eunice invites readers into her life growing up in an immigrant family and the church. Being a pastor's kid meant she excelled as a taskmaster at home, a student at school, and a role model at church. Lee's vulnerability and courage in sharing her particular and ubiquitous stories are sacred gifts for Asian American Christian women and beyond. Her journey of deconstructing internalized perfectionism is inspiring. This memoir is a page-turner."

—YOUNG LEE HERTIG, author of *The Tao of Asian American Belonging: A Yinist Spirituality*

"I can appreciate why the Lord has invited Eunice to write *More Christ, More Me* because her story of overcoming unhealthy enmeshment to embrace a healthier differentiation is one that many others could benefit greatly from. In my honest opinion, her book should be required reading for any Asian American or Korean American in seminary, serving in a church, and even already leading or pastoring. Her honesty and depth of reflection are a breath of fresh air."

—KEN FONG, Affiliate Associate Professor of Asian American Church Studies at Fuller Theological Seminary

More Christ, More Me

More Christ, More Me

One Woman's Spiritual Journey of Finding Her True Self

EUNICE LEE

Foreword by Judith Hong Cho

RESOURCE *Publications* · Eugene, Oregon

MORE CHRIST, MORE ME
One Woman's Spiritual Journey of Finding Her True Self

Resource Publications
An Imprint of Wipf and Stock Publishers
199 W. 8th Ave., Suite 3
Eugene, OR 97401

www.wipfandstock.com

PAPERBACK ISBN: 978-1-7252-9954-2
HARDCOVER ISBN: 978-1-7252-9955-9
EBOOK ISBN: 978-1-7252-9956-6

Unless otherwise indicated, all Scripture quotations are from the New Revised Standard Version Bible, copyright © 1989 National Council of the Churches of Christ in the United States of America. Used by permission. All rights reserved worldwide.

Scripture quotations marked NKJV are taken from the New King James Version®. Copyright © 1982 by Thomas Nelson. Used by permission. All rights reserved.

Scripture quotations marked NCV are taken from the New Century Version®. Copyright © 2005 by Thomas Nelson. Used by permission. All rights reserved.

Scripture quotations marked NIV are taken from the Holy Bible, New International Version®, NIV®. Copyright © 1973, 1978, 1984, 2011 by Biblica, Inc.™ Used by permission of Zondervan. All rights reserved worldwide. www.zondervan.com. The "NIV" and "New International Version" are trademarks registered in the United States Patent and Trademark Office by Biblica, Inc.™

09/09/21

For my parents, who loved me more than I understood.
For my birth mom. I can't wait to see you again someday.
For the One who called me.

Contents

Foreword

RECENTLY, I JOKED WITH friends who grew up in the same church as I did that the indoctrination happened early for us: "Children, obey your parents in the Lord, for this is right. 'Honor your father and mother'—which is the first commandment with a promise."[1] This was the very first Bible verse I committed to memory at the tender young age of five, and I would come to recite this verse every week at Sunday school and our church's Korean language school. We learned from the earliest days of our faith formation that being good children of God necessitated being good children to our parents. It was impossible not to conflate the two, and so honoring our parents became internalized as an integral element of a faithful Christian walk.

Apparently, this experience wasn't exclusive to my church. Eunice's story tells of her confrontation with this same belief as a young adult—that obedience to her parents and obedience to God were one and the same— and how this led to a spiritual crisis. It is a story I can find myself in.

Like Eunice, I too dearly loved and faithfully served the church that I called home for my whole life up through college. Like Eunice, I too faced unexpected opposition from spiritual authority figures when making a career decision that I thought was true to God's leading. When I shared my intent to move to Pasadena, California to attend Fuller Seminary, my kind, gentle-hearted senior pastor told me firmly that I was not to go. Instead, he told me to stay in Chicago and continue doing ministry for the children and youth (I was a volunteer, and the church had not replaced our previous children's pastor). My then boyfriend and his parents would have a different reaction, but no less upsetting. They sat me down and together with my church's former youth pastors (whom I had not even seen since I was a young girl) proceeded to tell me that if I was going to move to California, we should get married first because "anything can happen in a long-distance

1. Eph 6:1–2 (NIV).

relationship." Mind you, I was twenty-two, just finishing up college, and about to leave for graduate school in three months. Something deeply embedded—other than trust in my ability to discern God's next steps for my life or even their own trust in God's provision and plan for theirs—intertwined with their paradigm of Christianity, leading these authority figures to believe they had the right to dictate decisions I should have been making instead.

Eunice's process of healing sheds light on how easily and often something other than trust in God can shape the expectations and behavior of our faith communities. By dissecting the outside voices that influenced her understanding of God and herself, her book illustrates how important it is to understand that some of the beliefs about God we take for granted are neither absolute nor consistent with the gospel. As a psychotherapist who has counseled a diverse range of clients from all different ethnic and social backgrounds, it is clear to me that Eunice's story speaks to the broader-reaching truths of relational dynamics that exist in every family system and church. It is at once personally resonant and widely relatable across cultures and perhaps even faith traditions.

When I first met Eunice at Fuller, she was in the School of Theology and I was in the School of Psychology pursuing a master's in marriage and family therapy. Our connection was immediate (perhaps it was the Korean concept of *jeong*, or perhaps it was because she is simply one of the most genuine, easy-to-love people you'll ever meet); we quickly bonded over all we had in common. We reflected on spirituality, women in ministry, and our experiences in an immigrant church (as well as volleyball, boyfriends, the merits of hamburgers vs. cheeseburgers . . .).

Seminary was also a place where our thoughts on theology—who God is and who God calls us to be—were expanded, challenged, and even blown up at times. We explored together the coexistence and intersection of faith, theology, the church, mental health, family dynamics, justice, culture, and so on. These intersections were often in tension with one another, as this was the messy work of integration—what I believe forms a more holistic faith. Eunice and I were not always on the same page, as we were on our own individual trajectories of wrestling with what we thought we knew about Jesus and the Scriptures. But I am certain we were always mutually enriched. Through those conversations, this psychology student and that theology student engaged in the process of deconstructing and reconstructing deeply rooted elements of our faith, whether we realized it or not, and we grew toward fuller identities and a healthier faith.

By sharing her story, Eunice invites readers into this same process of growth, integration, and even healing. To reflect on how perhaps their own family and cultural dynamics—even those taught to them by the church—could be impeding their faith development. She also demonstrates how to deconstruct and reconstruct these elements in order to flourish in a God-given identity. This book is a courageous story about finding one's authentic self within the context of our complex human relationships—without cutting ourselves off from or staying fused with those we are connected to. Eunice's journey tells of the hope and possibility within each of us of coming into truer versions of ourselves—who God desires us to be. And it encourages us to believe that dynamic shifts can occur in our relationships with God and others when we bravely lean into our truths.

Ultimately, I believe this is a story of discipleship—of a disciple, finding her voice, finding her way. And her journey illuminates a path for others, like you and me, to do the same.

Acknowledgments

THIS BOOK COULDN'T HAVE come together without the support of many. Thank you to . . .

My partner in life, John Lee. I love you more and am more grateful for you with each passing year. You are my greatest teammate and wise sounding board. You encouraged me in this project from the beginning, when it was just an idea. You give me freedom to be myself, you challenge me to grow, and you are my strong guard.

My beta readers for their time and feedback: Mary, Gina, Lisa, Judith. Alex for being insulted that I didn't ask him to be a beta reader and volunteering himself. Camila for offering the perspective of her generation—seeing you explore and find your own path is my joy and even my inspiration. Especially Hannah for our many text conversations, for patiently helping me think through various mental tangles, for pushing me gently to step beyond my comfort zone, and for being my informal publicist.

The trailblazers who have gone before and shared their hard-earned gains with those who follow. Dr. Ken Fong for offering to read my manuscript and generously making his personal connection with his publisher available to me when he met me for the first time and I had barely written a word—and making good on that six years later when I finally had a manuscript. You made publishing seem like an attainable goal, and that kept me going. Dr. Young Lee Hertig for liberally sharing her time and wisdom from her own publishing experience and reminding me to celebrate each step taken throughout the process.

Fuller Theological Seminary and the professors who taught me to think in terms of both-and, not just either/or, and to sit in tension. Dr. David Augsburger for his gentle, wise, and formational teaching.

Ki and Katie Pyon, also known as JDSN and SMN, for giving me the tools to know God for myself and for investing in me.

All my dear friends for prayers and encouragement, and for processing everything life throws at us with me. You know who you are.

My therapist, Dr. Andrea Davis, who took me on as a client even when she technically had no room for more. And four years later, here we are. I'm so much healthier and happier, more confident, more at peace, and more differentiated due to your skill and presence. Therapy helps me put my experience into words, and many of those words have ended up in the following pages. You believed in this book and in me from the beginning, even taking on the role of an informal book agent during some of our sessions. Everyone needs a Dr. Davis in their life!

My family for giving me content to write a book. I kid. I love and appreciate my family so much that words aren't sufficient. We've been through a lot, we've all changed and grown, and the way we genuinely care for one another is incredibly precious to me.

And of course, the triune God. I am because you are. May your loving and communal presence abide in me more and more. I love you; thank you for loving me first.

Introduction

ONE DAY AS I drove my friend to LAX airport at the end of her visit, we were engaged in a frequent topic of discussion: the tension between doing what we wanted with our lives and what our first-generation Korean immigrant parents wanted us to do. Added to this was the complication that our faith dictated that we honor our parents, even though sometimes God's leading seemed to contradict what our parents wanted.

I attempted to explain to her how a single class at Fuller Seminary changed the way I saw my interactions with my parents and helped lessen my fear of making them unhappy. This had given me the freedom to live the life I wanted, but at the same time enabled me to communicate and connect with my parents more deeply. The class changed my whole life.

On my way home, now alone, I mulled over our conversation and wished that people in a similar situation—torn between the expectations of family and culture on the one hand, and what we feel is our true selves on the other—could have access to the new framework and insights I had learned. I also wished I could've expressed them to my friend in a clearer, more organized, and more digestible way. The idea of writing a book to fulfill these wishes crept into my mind.

Initially, I pushed it away. But the thought persisted. When it seemed confirmed that this idea came from God, I took the plunge and started. Through a laborious process of wrangling my chaotic thoughts into a coherent, presentable form, here it is—finished.

This book consists of three main parts: construction, deconstruction, and restoration. The first tells the story of how my background as a pastor's kid (PK) in a Korean American church and my earliest spiritual experiences formed my theology and understanding of my identity. Hence, construction.

The second part addresses how that theology became limiting as I ran into that very paradox of believing God both wanted me to obey my parents and was guiding me to do something contrary to their wishes. I summarize what I learned from my class Family Therapy and Pastoral Counseling and explain how it helped me to evaluate those theological limitations. I discuss how some ideas desperately needed to be dissolved and others reframed in order to move forward. Hence, deconstruction.

The third part covers how this revised framework provided me with a new way to relate to my parents and be in the world—something I badly needed, as I kept falling into patterns of burnout. It changed the way I engaged in the church and my communities because I was able to depend less on outside voices to establish my worth. Hence, restoration.

At the end of each section, I include reflection questions because I hope that my theological development and shifts can help bring awareness to your own story—your theological foundation and how it colors your self-perception, how much you depend on external influences to determine your value and purpose, and, perhaps, what aspects you need to release.

I conclude with an epilogue that is essentially a reflection on leadership in the church and a call for action to leaders—because healthy leaders are so crucial for healthy people. As a bonus, there is an appendix that lists resources and some helpful tips.

One note I'd like to make is that I deeply love my parents, if that's not obvious. I honor who they are and what they have persevered through. My story is told from my perspective, and if given the opportunity, they might tell a story that differs from mine.

In the past several years, I have had incredible, open, and healing conversations with them. When they visited LA or I visited them in Seattle, I subjected them to the latest revelations I had had in therapy about our family and my relationship with them. At the beginning, my mom asked me, "Why do you keep bringing up the past? That was then, and now we're so much better!" I explained to her that even if my adult mind can understand my parents' perspectives and intentions now—even if we're okay now—my inner child experienced and interpreted past events a certain way, which continued to influence my sense of security and self-understanding. This was manifesting itself as anxiety and insecurity in present-day situations, hampering my ability to live peacefully and confidently. For that reason, it was important to have the conversations so my inner child could voice her fears and learn important things: "Oh, Mom and Dad, you did love me, and not just based on my performance?" or, "Oh, that wasn't because you were ashamed of me? It was your own shame?"

Even the act of having these conversations retrained my brain and taught me the power of process in relationship—that conflict can actually be worked through, not just ignored. Being upset with each other didn't mean the relationship was over or that one of us was bad. I learned that our love for each other is strong enough to bear the difficult emotions. Saying awkward things out loud (like "Dad, when you say that, I hear, 'You're not good enough.' Is that what you mean?") has helped prevent internalization and reinforcement of damaging beliefs about myself. Now I know—not just cerebrally but in my body and heart—that my parents have my back and love me. We may not always agree, but the firm fact that they are my "backup," as Marcus says in *About a Boy*, provides me with strength and firm ground underfoot, and hope for the future. I will always be grateful for them.

Thank you for joining me on my journey! As you read my story, I pray that God speaks to you through it. I hope there are places where your story intersects with mine in timely and God-ordained ways so that you can find greater freedom to pursue who God has made you to be—not who others think you should be.

Part 1

Construction

After yet another tense day, I decided to attempt another conversation with my mom. My parents' bedroom stood only a few feet from my own, but a chasm of discord filled that space. I knew this was the time in the evening when my dad would continue to work in his office downstairs for the next couple of hours, and the light coming through their partially closed door indicated that my mom sat at her desk alone. Perhaps if I could speak with my mom and open my heart to her, she'd understand me and I wouldn't feel so weighed down by the distress of making my parents unhappy.

I decided to risk the chasm and take the leap. I could barely handle the stress as it was; something had to change or I was going to go crazy.

"Mom, can we talk?"

Sigh. "What do you want to talk about?"

"Could you pray with me?"

I thought that maybe if we prayed about this situation together, we'd be able to come to a place of understanding. After all, even if we disagreed about this, we had God in common, and God couldn't be of two different minds. If we sought God together, we had to come to a mutual conclusion.

She agreed. And prayed that God would change my mind.

That wasn't quite what I had envisioned. I thought maybe an open-ended petition to ask God to guide me would've been helpful, but clearly, she already had her answer. Her message rang loud and clear: I was very, very wrong.

After graduating college and spending the summer in Honduras on a mission trip, I returned home and began to search for full-time jobs. After all, for those who didn't intend on pursuing further education immediately, that was the normal and expected sequence of events after graduation.

However, as I explored jobs, submitted résumés, interviewed, and even received some offers, a sense of discontent and distaste persisted in the pit of my stomach. Every job description sounded stale and uninteresting, and in every interview, I silently rebelled as I told the interviewer why I would be great for the position and how eager I was for the opportunity. I felt like a puzzle piece being forced into a spot where it didn't belong, a square block being shoved into a circular hole. But I didn't know exactly what aspect of the job search repulsed me. Was it the idea of working in an office? Was it the need to sell myself at every interview? The wrong field? Unrealistic expectations? Business school had taught me how to manage projects, not push paper. Maybe I was disappointed at the entry-level positions, the reality of what was available to me without real work experience. Finally, I decided to step back from the job search in the hope of gaining some perspective.

"Okay," I told myself, "I know that when I'm doing something that God wants me to do, even if it's hard, there's at least a sense of peace, and it doesn't feel forced. I know that even if I don't want to do something and part of me resists, as long as I know God wants it, there's a satisfaction that supersedes that resistance. Then maybe this weird, icky feeling I'm having about job searching is telling me something. Either I'm doing what I'm supposed to be doing (and I'm just being a brat), or God actually does have something else in store for me. I mean, I've learned that I can trust that God has a plan for me. Shouldn't that extend to the job search as well? I simply want to be where God wants me to be, whether in an office cubicle or somewhere else. If there's a job out there for me, God knows what it is. I just need to wait and trust."

So I decided to pray and seek God's guidance. If I was being a brat, I asked God to convict me so that I could continue the job-search process without feelings of revulsion; if there was "something else," I asked God to reveal that and lead me. When I made this decision, I banked on the relationship I had established with God up to that point, one that had already gone through various growing pains that instilled in me deep confidence in God's faithfulness, guidance, and grace.

I was totally unprepared for the displeasure my decision evoked in my parents. They were dumbfounded and offered their own interpretation of the situation: I was being lazy and naïve. Still, I tried to persevere in my decision, convinced that God sanctioned what I was doing because my motivation was to do God's will and to trust no matter what. As long as I trusted God, things would work out, right?

However, that confidence diminished as the tension grew in our house. I found myself trying to do everything else I thought would please my parents in order to appease them, avoid any possibility of criticism, and maintain a tenuous balance—help around the house, be home for dinner, wake up early, earn money through tutoring, and obey them in every other respect—because putting my job search on hold was a ticking time bomb about to explode. Among my siblings, I had always had the most openly affectionate relationship with my parents, but soon, I couldn't approach my parents without caution and fear.

The night I asked my mom to pray with me was one of several conversations I tried to have in an attempt to bridge the growing rift between my parents and me. I wanted to explain to her my motives and make clear that I wasn't being lazy; I was actually willing to work. But these attempts usually escalated into my mom releasing her anger like a forceful river released from the shackles of a dam and left me backing away in tears. She could not comprehend my perspective.

"Pray?! Pray about whether you should look for a job? Of course you should look for a job! That's just what you do!"

"I don't understand how my smart and talented daughter is choosing not to work and instead is sitting at home playing!"

The worst was when my mom said, "People at church ask me, 'What's wrong with your daughter? Why isn't she working? Does she think you and Reverend are so wealthy that she doesn't need to work?' I have no answer for them."

It came to a point where I simply couldn't handle it anymore. Even though it didn't altogether make sense even to me, I genuinely felt that God told me the course I had chosen was right. At the time, I was reading daily from the book of Jeremiah, and while I couldn't claim to be on anywhere near the same footing as the prophet, I noted repeatedly how Jeremiah was persecuted by his own people and told he was completely mistaken about what God was saying. All the other prophets in Judah proclaimed that God would free the nation from its attackers, while Jeremiah alone declared that it would be destroyed and the people taken captive. Jeremiah stood alone but stayed the course because he knew his word came from God.

It seemed like a parallel scenario, albeit mine was of slightly lesser cosmic proportion. However, I also knew that if there was any false motive in me, it could easily cloud my discernment of God's word. I kept asking myself if I was manipulating God's word to my own situation to hear what I wanted and not truly God's voice: "Am I being lazy? Am I just shirking responsibility? Do I expect other people to work hard so I can have it easy?" I sifted through my own motives over and over until I was mentally exhausted and spiritually raw, like open blisters on my feet being continuously rubbed by a pair of brand-new, too-small stilettos.

So when my mom attacked my motives once again, believing more in the doubts of church members than in her daughter, I broke. My parents thought I was indolent and selfish; church members thought I was a leech; my siblings and friends were uncertain. And God didn't seem to be doing anything. No comforting presence, no reassuring peace. Perhaps the passages from Jeremiah should've been enough, but they seemed like very little to stand on when I couldn't even be sure of my own motives and everyone else imputed folly to me. I must be wrong. I had to be wrong. I made myself be wrong.

Alone in my dark bedroom, heart in agony, I conducted an ominous transaction in which I squelched all independent thought until it became nothing. I sat myself down, looked myself in the eye, and said deliberately and firmly, "What you think doesn't matter. You. Are. Wrong."

I told myself, "Apparently, all that matters is that I get a job. It doesn't matter what job, just *a* job, because that's the only thing that is right in the eyes of everyone."

When I woke up the next morning, I hurled myself recklessly into searching for jobs, not even caring what the positions were but applying to anything and everything. It was late afternoon when I received a text from my friend: "Hey, I know you're not looking for jobs right now, but my brother-in-law really needs someone. Would you be interested?"

Coincidence?

I responded, "Actually, I literally just started looking for jobs again today, so yes, I am interested."

I turned in my résumé, interviewed the next day, and received an offer that same day. In fact, I barely interviewed because the manager had already heard about me from my friend and felt satisfied with her report. I asked more questions than he did. Before I knew it, I was installed as a customer accounts manager at a small company in the U District. It happened in such dizzying haste that I had even forgotten to give notice to a family whose daughter I was tutoring. It wasn't until the day of her lesson that I realized my negligence. I had to call her from the office and apologetically inform her I wouldn't be able to tutor her that day or ever again. That's how much the rush of events bewildered me.

My procurement of a job instantly restored my footing in society, as well as peace and calm to my household. My relationship with my parents returned to some semblance of normalcy. Outwardly, I was now the proper daughter and human being that everyone expected me to be, giving my parents no need to evade questions or explain halfheartedly and shamefacedly what I was doing.

But at what cost?

Internally, I was desolate, as well as psychologically and spiritually broken. The seemingly divine timing—the job opportunity coinciding with my submission to my parents by resuming the job search—appeared to confirm that I had, in fact, been wrong all along, and everyone else had been right. Worst of all, it appeared that God too agreed that I was a foolish little girl who just needed to get a job.

My relationship with God became a shadow of what it formerly was. I had been "running the race,"[1] trying my best to be faithful to God's will, but then I was violently blindsided off the track. Now I lay on the ground, bruised and bloody and smeared with dirt, and when I looked up to see who had done it, I saw God. It seemed like God had punished me for trying to follow God.

I felt betrayed and confused. As life moved on irrespective of my internal tempest, I continued to insist on God's goodness and loving nature in my mind, even teaching and affirming it to others; but in my heart, I was deeply afraid to trust God again. I no longer felt sure that God was who I had thought God was.

1. Heb 12:1.

1

The Perfect Child

PERFECTIONIST. TEACHER'S PET. GOODY Two-shoes. OCD. Overachiever. These are the labels I wore growing up—given to me by others and also by myself. Although some are not so flattering, they convey an idea of what kind of person I was as a child and adolescent. It wasn't that I *wanted* to be a teacher's pet. Who wants that? But I thought it was odd to be teased for doing the right thing, to be made to feel wrong for doing right. I suppose the fact that I found this strange maybe reveals even more about me. I had a sensitive conscience as a child, and I guess you could say—for better and for worse—that my parents did an excellent job of drilling into me a deep-seated respect for authority, rules, and high standards. This was especially the case with anything God-related: nothing was more important than implicit obedience in every respect.

Growing up, my parents were strict, particularly compared to my white friends' parents. School activities were automatically allowed and encouraged, but the opposite was true for social events. Events that were a matter of course for my friends, like sleeping over at each other's houses, were rarely permitted. And you can imagine my shock in elementary school when I learned that my neighborhood friends were rewarded with money for earning 3s (out of 4) on their report cards. At my house, 4s were simply expected, and my parents would ask me why the two 3s that showed up on mine weren't 4s.

As children, when we thought we were simply explaining our perspective, our parents viewed it as talking back, which was met with zero tolerance. Though I was never grounded (an American concept foreign to my parents), they had a far more effective tool: the *mongdongee*. This was a wooden rolling pin (which I didn't even realize at the time was a rolling pin) used to strike my hands or the bottom of my feet with the intent of nipping any rebellion in the bud.

Some kids know they can manipulate their parents and get what they want by crying. But if *I* started crying, my dad would threaten to bring out the *mongdongee*. Of course, this would just make me want to cry more, but the fear of the *mongdongee* made me do my best to gulp down the tears. Unsurprisingly, I quickly learned to adopt the value of obedience without question or complaint.

But even more potent than the *mongdongee* in teaching me standards for behavior was seeing the way my parents self-disciplined themselves to live out this value of obedience. As a pastor and pastor's wife, their time and energy were consumed with serving the church in absolute dedication to God. This was the driving force of their identities.

Sunday services and other church gatherings composed a natural part of the rhythm not only of the weekend but of everyday life. My parents often had evening commitments connected with the church: *shimbang* (visitations to church members' homes), *sooyo yaebae* (Wednesday night service), *jeonyeok yaebae* (Sunday night service) or *seonggyeong gongboo* (Bible study). Sitting down to dinner as a family took place daily, but also regular were the sounds of my parents rushing through it to get ready to go out. I'd hear my dad's reminder of "Hurry, *yeobo* (honey), it's already 7:00" if my mom was caught up in conversation; the clanking of their dishes as they put them in the sink; the brushing of teeth and gargling of water; their feet clattering down the stairs and the thumping of shoes being set down and slipped on; the bang of the front door behind them; the car engine starting and driving away; and then an ensuing calm silence. *Saebyuk gido* (early-morning prayer service) also meant they were up at 5:00 a.m. every day and back just in time for my mom to get ready to take the bus downtown for work. No matter how tired or even sick my parents were, there was virtually no excuse that could justify missing church.

I always believed my dad was fairly unique as far as pastors (especially Korean ones) go in that he really made an effort to be present with us. He regularly attended our school events and took our family on trips—but we always planned around church. One summer during a road trip, our tan VW Vanagon broke down. My parents fretted about finding a mechanic and getting it fixed in time for us to return home by Saturday night. Having already missed the midweek Wednesday service for this vacation, their anxiety and stress over the possibility of missing a Sunday service on top of that—even due to circumstances outside our control—hung over us like a dark cloud.

With me too my parents enforced the priority of church over other activities. Every summer, my friend invited me to a weekend getaway at her cabin for her birthday. To be included in her circle thrilled me because she was decidedly all-American cool. It felt as if I had arrived socially but then was always teetering on the fringes of the danger zone because I was never allowed to go. That same friend invited me to play on a basketball team coached by her parents. As usual, the first question I had to ask was when the games were. Although most games fell on Saturdays, the season always included two Sunday games. Upon learning this, I saw all my NBA dreams come crashing down . . . (Clearly I joke, but the fear that this would prevent me from joining the team at all was very real!) With trepidation, I asked my parents if I could miss church for those games. Predictably, they said no before the question was even fully out of my mouth, it seemed. Church was an absolute, and serving God came first before our desires and convenience.

My mom embodied the ideal Korean *sahmonim* (pastor's wife), meaning she was a paragon of self-denial and sacrifice. She essentially had three full-time jobs: mom and wife (wait, those alone could almost count as two . . .), paralegal, and *sahmonim* (yes, that's right, I did just qualify it as a full-time job). Her duty to family and the church always came before her own needs. My dad's salary as a pastor didn't leave much margin with four kids, so my mom spent a weary thirty-eight years at the same law firm as a paralegal to support our family and give us opportunities (like piano lessons we didn't appreciate at the time or continue). My dad loves to tell the story about how my mom dreamed of being able to take our family to Disneyland (imagine paying for a family of six!), and by saving up meticulously, they did it—twice!

My parents tended toward traditional Korean gender roles, so my mom did all the cooking and my older sisters helped her with the housecleaning—leaving my dad more available for ministry. I can speak to this myself now that I am married: preparing a traditional Korean dinner night in and night out is no joke (and something I've long given up on trying to do)! Each meal consists of rice, various side dishes, a form of protein, and a soup or stew. Somehow, this is something that my mom delivered every day without fail, preparing the night before and finishing up as soon as she came home from the office.

Then she'd turn around and get ready for church or a visitation in the evening—and don't forget that she had already gone to early morning prayer service and was going again the next day! She faithfully attended every church event, managed relationships with various church members (including long phone conversations putting out fires and listening to troubles and complaints), strove to set an example for all church members, and maintained her personal spiritual disciplines of daily Bible study and prayer.

I still remember hearing my mom earnestly praying in my parents' room during evenings at home. If my dad was away at a revival and my mom couldn't go with him, she would intercede for him throughout the entire time he was scheduled to speak.

My mother's capacity to labor, serve, and sacrifice unceasingly astounds me—more so now that I am older and can grasp the extent of all she did. She just gave and gave and gave. And worked and worked and worked. And what is remarkable is that this was *normal* to her, not anything exceptional.

Led by my parents' example, I sought to present myself as a model Christian who not only went to church regularly but also knew the Bible thoroughly, didn't say bad words, acted kindly toward others, and respected those who were older. Dutifully, I raised my hand to every question in Sunday school to display my biblical prowess while trying to ignore the other kids' faces that clearly expressed, "Of course, Eunice"; diligently showed deference to the adults by bowing and using *jeondeamahl* (formal speech); conscientiously recited my memory verses each week; sang as loudly as I could during special programs; sat quietly during service even as other kids fooled around; and, while the other kids wore ordinary T-shirts and jeans, donned a dress every Sunday at my parents' behest (because "one must give one's best to God")—basically branding PASTOR'S KID on my forehead.

But somewhere along the way, obedience to God and being a good Christian melded together with pleasing others and fulfilling their expectations. In a way, gaining others' approval became a proxy for doing right in the eyes of God.

Other church members constantly scrutinized my siblings and me and expected us, as pastor's children, to set an example for our peers. We were continually aware that to them, our behavior reflected on our parents and any missteps would give ammunition to the elders to criticize them.

Parents at church would also use me as leverage with their kids, attempting to pressure them to behave a certain way. I can see how that would annoy my friends—but they also did the same thing in reverse. If I was allowed to do something (attend a school dance, for example), they would leverage that to convince their parents to let them do likewise. Surely if the pastor let his daughter go to a dance, it must be okay. (Of course, my dad allowed me to go to dances only when I had to go as a class officer, which was once a year. Anything school-related was always approved.)

Ironically, even though it was impressed on me to make decisions without comparing myself to others, I was continually judged by comparison. This constant expectation to behave differently and "better" created a lot of pressure for my entire family.

Unfortunately, my parents reinforced this anxiety for approval. One time, my mom stopped me as I carried a used Nordstrom bag with clothes to change into after church and told me to change the bag. If church members saw me with a Nordstrom bag, they would say our family must be rich—and a pastor's family shouldn't be wealthy. This conveyed to me that I wasn't only supposed to conduct myself in a way that was right in God's eyes, but also in a way that was right in other people's eyes. Maybe I wasn't supposed to be influenced by how others acted, but I *was* supposed to be influenced by what they thought.

Given these kinds of expectations and my upbringing, perhaps those labels that I shared at the beginning of this chapter aren't so surprising.

There were, of course, times when the benchmarks felt grossly unfair and annoying. But I accepted them as what a good Christian should do and held myself to those standards. After all, wasn't pleasing my parents pleasing God? Didn't God, in fact, deserve my best? So I did do the best I could by seeking to perform as an ideal daughter and Christian, which also meant being an ideal student, friend, leader—really, the ideal person. This became my identity. I had to be perfect in the eyes of everyone.

It started out all right. If there was any kind of measurement involved, I resolved to choose the hardest path and achieve at the highest level, with no compromise. I mean, it wasn't just my parents who wanted all 4s on my report card. For me, those two 3s were deeply unsettling and broke the satisfying consistency of that column of 4s.

In fourth grade when I watched my oldest sister graduate with a 4.0 as the valedictorian of her class, I determined I would do the same in high school. In sixth grade while registering for middle-school classes for the first time, a note at the bottom of the sheet caught my eye. I could start with algebra (which usually began in ninth grade) if my teacher expressed confidence in my ability to succeed at that level. I immediately sought out my teacher and eagerly asked her to sign the sheet. Even though middle-school grades didn't matter for college, I was still determined to get that 4.0, and did it.

But as I entered high school, the strenuous effort to maintain my perfect image began to wear me down as the expectations intensified. My school offered the International Baccalaureate (IB) diploma program, which was more involved and challenging than the Advanced Placement (AP) program. AP consisted of college-level curricula for which one could later receive college credit. IB included this too, but then piled additional requirements on top, such as community service, a research paper, unique classes like Theory of Knowledge, and select essays and projects sent to the IB headquarters in Switzerland for assessment. While I could have settled for certificates in chosen subjects—which paralleled more closely with the

AP program—the IB *diploma* was the highest, most difficult curriculum my school offered. *Of course* I had to do it, while still pursuing that perfect 4.0 and valedictorian status.

This by itself would've been enough to keep me busy, but other activities quickly filled up every spare moment. Typically, students had three classes a day on an alternating schedule (for a total of six classes), and they either started early and ended early or started late and ended late. However, as a class officer, I was required to take the leadership class and also opted to take orchestra as an elective. This meant that I both started early and ended late, with an extra class each day. After my last class of the day, walking down the stairs toward the gym, I would see the crowd of my volleyball teammates boisterously pouring out from the common area. I couldn't help but envy how they had just enjoyed one hundred delightfully free minutes waiting for practice to start.

On game days, it wasn't unusual to return home around 9:00 p.m. I'd bolt down some food and then start my homework-on-steroids. IB classes usually demanded a little something extra to secure the A, like reading an additional historian, taking notes, and writing supplementary commentary on those notes. Often, I'd fall asleep over my textbooks and wake up with a jolt at 3:00 a.m. to start again. Most nights, I slept only three to four hours, and all-nighters became all too common.

I also had the added responsibilities of being a class officer. While the leadership class was designed to provide time to have meetings and make event posters, there were always some activities that had to take place outside of class. Homecoming guaranteed nights of scant sleep as we ramped up for the festivities and prepared our class parade float, banner, and skit. Throughout the year, we held fundraisers and other events, like the class-hosted dance. Naturally, my orchestra concerts always managed to happen during the busiest times. And to top it off, I held a part-time job during my sophomore and junior years.

None of this, of course, excused me from church responsibilities, just as church never gave me an excuse to study less. Weekends offered little respite from my frenetic pace due to those commitments: Saturday night Bible study, a youth group event or meeting, praise band practice, and Sunday service. As a youth-group officer, I worked with other leaders to plan outings and fundraisers. We researched venues and prices, coordinated rides, and called members throughout the week to see if they could make it (in the days before cell phones and texting). Sometimes, we even prepared the Bible studies. On Sundays, I arrived early to set up and warm up with the praise band, and we often held officer meetings after service.

Sitting here now, I can't imagine how I fit it all in. I'm pretty sure I got through high school on pure adrenaline. To this day, if I'm particularly stressed out, I have nightmares of being back in high school, having forgotten to study for a test or not knowing which classes I have that day.

Let me tell you, college was a *breeze* in comparison. I basked in the bliss of being able to simply read textbooks without having to take notes. I'm not complaining; I had a lot of fun along the way, and I learned a lot about responsibility, leadership, character, and perseverance. But I was also incredibly stressed out and tired. It often reached a point where I felt completely overwhelmed, like I would unravel. But the drive to be perfect prevented me from seeking any kind of reprieve.

I remember showing up late to calculus (more than once), my first period of the day. Rushing through the eerily quiet hallways with my hair still dripping from my shower and backpack laden with books, juggling a sports bag and violin, out of breath, homework barely done—it was a perfect representation of my chaotic, slipping-through-my-fingers life. The very fact that I was late mortified me, a public falling short of perfection. I think my math teacher (who was truly great) took one look at my harried state and had pity on me, because he never made me feel ashamed for being late or ridiculous for my appearance. At most, he made a lighthearted joke. I thought the whole world could tell I was ready to crack, but I always put on my brightest smile to make it look like I had everything under control. Little did everyone know how many times I thought I would fall to pieces because of how exhausted and stretched thin I felt, and how terrified I was of dropping the ball in one area of my life and seeing everything else come crashing down. I would have to admit in front of everyone, "*I can't do this.*"

I suppose that in theory, I could have simply accepted a B or let go of some extracurricular activities. However, in my reality, a B meant failure, and playing sports and holding leadership positions at school and church offered me the assurance of being "well-rounded"—an important quality in my conception of an ideal person.

And it's not that simple once people know you a certain way.

After building a reputation as smart, talented, and reliable, it felt as if there were more at stake if I failed. A friend gave me the nickname "Ms. Perfect," and one of our graduation speakers even referenced me in his speech and asked, "Is there anything you don't do?" While they meant it as a compliment, all of this made me fearful: What if I made a mistake and exposed myself as less than perfect?

The more I succeeded, the deeper I dug myself into a hole and felt trapped. As the gap widened between people's perceptions and the real me, the scarier it became to do anything that might alter their impression. The more I committed to, the more people seemed to increasingly depend on me and expect certain things, further heightening the risk of disappointing them.

I learned to hide when I was having a hard time, and one of my go-to expressions at the time was "Suck it up." I told myself, "You have a lot to do—so what? Everyone does." Nothing was going to get accomplished by having a pity party. There was no time to stop. I had to move with the rushing stampede or get trampled. After all, revealing my struggles would be admitting weakness, staining my flawless image. So on the outside, I continued to look like I had it all together.

Besides stress and sleep deprivation, this led to other problems: a guilt complex, a gulf of insecurity, and a feeling of emptiness. My sense of worth depended upon being perfect, and being perfect hinged on my ability to perform and fulfill others' expectations. The moment I did something short of perfect—which inevitably happened—it threw me into a storm of self-condemnation, and I felt the need to make up for it, almost like paying a penance. If someone asked for a favor that I didn't have time for or simply didn't want to do, I would feel too guilty to say no. I gave in out of fear and then immediately felt guilty for not helping them with a good attitude. This, in turn, led to additional problems, like resentment and feeling taken advantage of. It was a vicious cycle.

But no matter how many friends I had or accomplishments I could claim, a question ate at me in the back corner of my mind: am I loved for who I really am or just for what I show myself to be? I asked myself, "What if they knew I'm not actually perfect? Would people still like me if they knew my weaknesses, the parts I try to conceal? What would they think of me if I failed? Am I _____ (fill in the blank: pretty, smart, athletic, likeable, good) enough?" But perhaps the scariest question of all was this: "If I'm not as perfect as I try to appear, then who am I?"

Because I was driven to please others in the midst of such intense busyness, life became a mechanical process of going through the motions. And survival.

What was it all for anyway? Going and going without stopping to reflect upon *why* I was doing any of these things . . . I felt empty. I didn't want to continue mindlessly going through the motions; life had to be more than that.

What started out as learning to obey my parents and God had morphed into a compulsion to please others, resulting in an exhausting merry-go-round of self-doubt, pressure, anxiety, and fear. Thankfully, even as I became aware of these realities, at the same time God was showing me that this was not God's desire for me at all. Genuine obedience to God actually led to much better things than these.

2

Learning to Love God

EVEN AS I SOUGHT to please my parents according to a religion I had inherited from them, the consciousness of a need to form my own faith decision emerged as early as elementary school. I asked myself then, "Is this something that *I* really believe or something that I just say I believe because my parents told me to?"

As a kid, in the early stages of my faith, God was one among many people to please, often mirroring the desires of my parents. During middle school, however, the fact that Jesus died on the cross for my sins—a concept Christians can sometimes mindlessly regurgitate as a Sunday-school lesson—became deeply meaningful and personal to me.

In high school, the growth of my faith accelerated as I turned to prayer and the Bible to cope with the mounting expectations and my struggle with insecurity. I began to recognize, at least mentally, that God was the *only* person to please. One of the stories that shifted the way I related to God was the story of David.

Many people know David for killing Goliath and becoming the king of Israel. But what amazed me most was that God called David a man after God's own heart. The sharp contrast between David and Saul, God's first chosen king, highlighted this. The Bible made sure to point out that Saul *looked* kingly—literally a head and shoulders above everyone—but God ultimately rejected him because he cared more about appearance and reputation than about honoring and obeying God. On the other hand, David was a virtual nobody, unimpressive and overlooked compared to his brothers. But as the story tells us, although people look at the outward appearance, God looks at the heart.[1] God saw in David a heart that pleased God, a heart that would honor God before himself.

This made me pause and consider: What about me? Did I only look like a good Christian and a good person but, like Saul, actually care more about myself than God? The answer was only too obvious.

I've already outlined in the previous chapter how my intense drive to be perfect developed into a need to please others. Others' approval mattered as much, if not more, to me than God's approval. But God took it even deeper. God showed me how this need to please others was not altruistic but instead a form of self-preservation. If people thought well of me, I felt good about myself; if they thought poorly of me, I felt bad about myself. I wanted to avoid that pain, and this led me to allow others' opinions to define me.

Among my peers, I had a reputation of being one of the nicest people. While I really did try to be kind, it wasn't always sincere. I knew better than anyone (except God, who often revealed to me motives I didn't even know I had) what lurked beneath the surface of my "goody-goody" exterior. Insecurity, fear, jealousy, selfishness, pride, arrogance, impatience, judgment, anger—it was all there. And underlying all of this was self-centeredness.

If I was jealous of someone or resisted giving a compliment, it was because I wanted what they had or didn't want others to like them better than me. If I was ungenerous, it was because I was scared of not having enough for myself. If I boasted or craved attention, it was because I feared being passed over. If I didn't befriend those who were unpopular, it was because I worried about my social status or didn't want to hamper my own fun. If I agonized over the college application process (which I did), it was due to anxiety about the reactions of teachers and peers who had voted me "Most Harvard-Bound" in our senior yearbook. If I became angry and couldn't stop talking back to my siblings, it was because I hated being wrong. If I was impatient with or critical of others, it was because I thought I could do better. Behind many modest smiles when people marveled at how I had aced another test was an attitude of arrogance and condescension, as well as a need to fill a void of insecurity. It was all about me.

In contrast, according to the story of David, the kind of person God wanted me to be had more to do with my heart than my outward appearance. Good deeds with selfish or sinful motivations were still essentially wrong. The obedience that God approved of encompassed the motivations behind those actions, even my most secret inner thoughts. And the kind of motivations God looked for was nothing slight. It entailed no less than

---

1. 1 Sam 16:7.

desiring what God desired, loving what God loved, and most of all, loving God more than anyone or anything else—even one's own self.

This was why God loved David so much. David's motivation behind his obedience was not obligation but rather a deep passion for God and the desire to stay intimately connected. As evident in his psalms, David experienced the presence of God, and nothing could compare to it. He longed for the personal presence of the Lord, which satisfied him more than any other person, object, or dream ever could. It was for this reason that he sought to obey the Lord and put sin far away. No one else's opinion mattered more to him.

Confronted by this truth, I realized that God's standard for perfection and righteousness was far more stringent than any grading rubric or social norm. It was much easier to exude a pristine image than to have a truly pure heart. However, even after realizing what God required and wanted from me, and even though I wished I loved God so much that I chose obedience gladly like David, I couldn't quite get there. At most, I did it out of duty or to look good in front of others.

This troubled me because I was serious about being a Christian and knew that meant I should obey God. Believing in God and obeying God went hand in hand. If I believed God existed, then I also had to obey and follow God. But while I could obey to a certain extent in my actions, this deeper area of inner intentions was an unruly jungle. Loves and desires don't simply change for the asking, no matter how rational the reason. At the end of the day, my self-centered motivations persisted. I still cared so much more about myself than God, and I definitely couldn't say that I *enjoyed* doing God's will.

Yet surprisingly, this awareness of my inability to meet this more exacting standard didn't result in a greater pressure to perform. In fact, its effect was quite the opposite: it set me free.

As I more clearly understood the true condition of my heart in light of David's story, it brought a keener understanding of and appreciation for God's grace. Even as God revealed deeper sin in me than I had ever realized, God didn't abandon me to figure it out on my own. Nor did God stand condemningly over me with crossed arms, saying, "Look at how bad you are; now show me what you're going to do about it." God the Father sent Jesus on my behalf to do what I couldn't do.

As a high school student, summer retreats and revivals were a huge highlight socially but also provided space for intense, deep spiritual experiences. In these settings, as I grappled with the stress and pressures of trying to be perfect, words that I had heard all my life as a regular churchgoer struck me to the core in a new way. That God demonstrated God's love for us through the cross "while we still were sinners" didn't make any sense;[2] it completely defied the pattern of love that I'd seen in the world. It's always easier to like someone who likes you first and to give once you see how much another person is willing to give. In my insecurity, I typically felt out people's responses before deciding the degree of warmth I showed them. How many times did I see high school couples get together because one person found out the other liked them, which usually provided a good enough incentive to reciprocate?

Yet here was God—who knew everything about me and could see all my flaws—laying it all out by declaring, "I love you and died for you to be close to you." The God of the universe took the risky first step to love me and give God's entire self, even though it only made sense for me to naturally adore God first. And the craziest part: *there was no guarantee that I would love God back.* This was akin to the most popular, good-looking boy in school declaring his love for me, the insecure, overlooked plain Jane. This was every teenage rom-com narrative come to life on a cosmic scale.

Not only that, but it was also a matter of betrayal—because essentially, sin is betrayal. Originally created to serve and love God, we turned our backs and sought other loves and our own way (evident in my own struggles as described earlier). While the cross demonstrated God's great love for me, it also clearly indicated that I was a sinner who, left to my own devices, would reject God.

Again, this kind of love made no sense to me. This wasn't just forgiveness for things like getting a B on a report card or missing serves in volleyball—which I thought I could lose other people's love over. It was forgiveness for my disloyalty to God and the real evil inside me. Justice, as we normally understand it, says that the betrayer should make amends or be punished. But God, out of abundant grace, pursued *me*, the traitor, and paid an immeasurably great cost to do so. It was as if I agreed to date the popular boy and then cheated on him with his best friend, but he tried to win me back before I showed any remorse or desire to be with him.

This conceptualization of God's love undid me. *Who does that?* Here I had been operating under the basic principle that I had to run after other people's love—somehow get them to love me and work to keep that love—by performing for them and preserving a perfect image. It was exhausting because it was so fragile and uncertain, something never quite fully attained and easily lost the moment you couldn't deliver. But God's love wasn't something that I could earn; it didn't depend on what I did—such sweet relief!

2. Rom 5:8.

And it was all the more solid, unchangeable, and dependable because it was given before I did anything for it—in fact, when I was at my worst.

The deeper I allowed the truth of God's love to sink into my soul, the more I was drawn in. I began to see God's amazing, beautiful worth and why David loved God so much. David understood the magnitude of God's love, mercy, and favor that was extended when he had done nothing to deserve it. It moved his soul to worship and love the Lord, to trust in God and willingly choose God's will over his own.

And there it was. Finally. My motives and desires actually began to change in the ways I couldn't make them before. I wanted to know God more, and a desire to please God welled up in my heart in response to this incredible love. I began to love God more truly and wanted to love to the degree God's worth warranted. But this did not result from greater effort on my part, by doing more; it came simply from experiencing God's love and grace extended to me through Christ in the face of my inadequacy.

It was quite the revelation. As a result, my theology underwent a drastic transformation: one fulfills God's standards simply by allowing oneself to be loved, by immersing oneself in God's good presence. So many things I had read in the Bible and learned in church started coming together and making sense. This is why Paul persistently insisted that nothing else mattered except for Christ and him crucified.[3] Paul declared that he had more reason to boast than others because of his many accolades, but it was all "loss because of the surpassing value of knowing Christ Jesus."[4] Knowing Christ was basically the key to—well, everything: the key to understanding the extent of God's love for me, the key to learning to love God more truly, the key to true righteousness.

Love truly is a great motivator—far better than force. Someone who does something because they have to will usually only do the bare minimum or, over time, become depleted. But someone who acts out of love gladly and willingly goes above and beyond. Even as they give and sacrifice, they are reenergized by the pleasure they are able to bring to the one they love, as well as by the love they continue to receive.

This kind of Christianity was so different from what I had been experiencing! It freed me on multiple levels. I had many conversations in high school about why I believed in God, sometimes having to defend my faith. But the most compelling reasons lay in the gospel itself—how it completely overturned the way any other system of the world operated.

3. 1 Cor 2:2.
4. Phil 3:8.

Conventional wisdom and evolution stated that you got what you deserved; those who came in first were the winners. You had to prove your worth by being the smartest, the most beautiful, the wealthiest, the most athletic, the most powerful, or the highest achiever. However, the gospel invited me to believe that my worth was intrinsic and to let myself be loved rather than try harder. God's beautiful love drew me in, and I couldn't help but love God in return.

3

Learning to Obey God

THOUGH IT MAY SEEM that my theology shifted in a moment and I changed overnight, it was actually a slow process for that theology to effect real changes in my life. Understanding God's love more and, in turn, loving God more in one moment didn't mean I was done for all time. It wasn't enough to make my heart instantly willing to obey God at all times or in every situation.

I was only willing to obey God insofar as I trusted in God's love for me. Unfortunately, I would frequently discover that while I *thought* I trusted God, I actually didn't in many ways. I grasped intellectually that God loved me as information learned and memorized. But I didn't always *feel* God's love and so didn't necessarily believe it to the fullest. Or I might trust God in one case but not in others. Often, what seemed more real was what I saw and felt.

It took God's discipline to teach me not to rely on my feelings but to trust God's word and to make God's love more than just something I understood cerebrally. It needed to be something I internalized and registered with my whole heart and soul, something I believed so much I could stake my life on it, as Jesus did. This discipline showed me that God was real, powerful, and in control, and that I could rely on God's character. Most of all, I could count on God's steadfast and unconditional love.

When I say discipline, I don't mean punishment. I did not see God as punitive at all. It was more like the discipline that an athlete or student exercises in order to improve and excel, and it took shape through difficult circumstances in my life. I don't mean to be dramatic; it's not as if my life was *so* hard. But I faced many of the challenges typical for any American teenager, and in the midst of these challenges, God instructed me to behave in direct contrast to how I felt like responding—adding further dimensions of difficulty.

For example, one thing I struggled with was my clothes. My mom didn't believe in spending a lot of money on clothes, and we lacked the means to keep up with the trends. While my friends' parents gave them hundreds of dollars for back-to-school shopping, this was a foreign concept to my mom. She viewed it as impractical to purchase new clothes when I already had clothes that still fit. I did the best I could with hand-me-downs, making new combinations with my old clothes and the two new items my oldest sister would buy for me. But my day-to-day self-consciousness over what I wore never left me.

An older girl from church once gave me her previously worn shirt. It didn't quite fit, so I never wore it by itself. It was a little tight and slightly short in the sleeves. To remedy this and avoid wasting a rare opportunity to supplement my wardrobe, I covered the torso with a fleece-lined vest and then wore wooly mittens that covered the ends of the sleeves (this was during winter), so the imperfect fit wasn't noticeable. I laughed to myself when a friend saw me wearing this outfit one day and exclaimed, "Gosh, Eunice, I love your style!" Then I would count the days until it was deemed socially appropriate to repeat an outfit before I wore the ensemble again.

Through Bible verses like Prov 31:30[1] and 2 Cor 4:17–18,[2] God showed me I shouldn't depend on my clothes or physical appearance to determine my worth. I should base it instead on what God valued, which was a person of character who feared God. God encouraged me to trust that even though I felt bad about my clothes at the moment, the unseen things—like character, faith, and how I loved others—were far more meaningful in the long run.

This was not easy. Although I tried to find comfort and strength in these verses, I still felt embarrassed at times and wished I could afford brand-name, stylish clothing. It was hard not to be envious of friends who never seemed to wear the same thing twice.

I also struggled when circumstances didn't work out the way I wanted. An example of this is when I applied to college. I desperately wanted to attend an out-of-state school and deliberately applied to only one school in

1. "Charm is deceitful, and beauty is vain, but a woman who fears the Lord is to be praised."

2. "For this slight momentary affliction is preparing us for an eternal weight of glory beyond all measure, because we look not at what can be seen but at what cannot be seen; for what can be seen is temporary, but what cannot be seen is eternal."

my home state as a backup—the University of Washington (UW). However, when the school counselor nominated me for a full-ride scholarship that could only be used in-state, I knew I couldn't pass up the opportunity. I told God, "You know how much I want to go to school out of state, but you also know how invaluable a full-ride scholarship would be to my family. I don't know which one to pray for, so I'm just going to put it in your hands."

A couple months later, it was announced that I had won the scholarship, and the moment I heard that news, it struck me as bittersweet. It was a great honor to win such a scholarship. Only three students out of each legislative district in Washington were chosen, and there was relief in knowing my entire college tuition was covered. However, my heart sank as I knew my decision had been made and I had to give up the coveted adventure of a new environment. To make matters worse, as if to seal the deal, I eventually discovered I hadn't gotten into a single school other than UW.

Did I wrestle with God a long time on that one. My attitude and emotions at that time were revealing. For one thing, they exposed my pride. I was mortified at the reality that I hadn't been accepted by any other school. To be capable of embarrassment means that one has pride, and it hurt my pride immensely to tell this news to my teachers and friends, especially because of their expectations for me.

But biblically speaking, although it hurt, I knew it wasn't terrible to be humbled because it taught me to depend on God's power and grace. On the one hand, winning the scholarship appeared to be a sign of my abilities. But at the same time, my rejection by every other school undercut any confidence in those abilities. It put me in a position where I couldn't take any credit for the outcome.

Throughout the Bible, I saw that God allowed circumstances to reach a point where only God could receive credit for a solution (such as Pharaoh refusing to let the Israelites go until God performed miracles through a scared and ineloquent Moses). God alone deserved and received the honor; and at the same time, great things happened for God's people—greater than they could ever have generated on their own. Through this lens, I concluded that to rely on myself would limit the space in which God's grace and power could work in my life.

Nonetheless, it was certainly difficult to trust that God was doing something good by closing the door on my dream of going out of state. Besides the obvious pride, my response also showed a lack of trust that God knew better than me and that God's plans for me were good. In that sense, it was another form of pride. I had said I was putting it into God's hands, but in reality, I was not prepared to be satisfied with just any result. I couldn't help asking God, "Why? Why did it have to be this way?" I thought I knew better what was good for my life.

I had read many times these verses: "For my thoughts are not your thoughts, nor are your ways my ways, says the Lord. For as the heavens are higher than the earth, so are my ways higher than your ways and my thoughts than your thoughts."[3] These words had always told me God saw and understood things that I couldn't. God's wisdom and perspective were superior to mine; thus, God's plans and purposes were also superior. I had made it my plan to attend school out of state, but apparently, that's not where I was meant to be. I had to have faith that the way things had worked out was indeed better, even if I couldn't see how.

I was presented with a choice to obey or not. Obedience meant trusting that God loved me, believing the things God said were truer than what I felt or saw, and relying on God's promises. Instead of embarrassment, envy, pride, or anger, I could choose to be confident, joyful, patient, and strong. Disobedience, on the other hand, meant succumbing to those feelings of mistrust and ignoring God.

Standing at this crossroads, the path toward trusting God felt *so* hard, while the other—giving in to my natural emotions—seemed so desirable and easy. Often, I would try to stay on that path of trust, but honestly, it felt like I was crawling inch by inch on my belly while complaining the whole way. Some days, I just wanted to give up.

Trusting in God during these times was made more difficult by God's apparent silence and distance. I couldn't feel God at all. There were certainly times when God seemed so real that I loved God with a fiery passion and was determined to live in full commitment. But those sensations would inevitably ebb away.

When God felt real, setting aside "quiet time" (QT) every morning was a delight. This was time spent with God through reading the Bible, praying, and journaling. It seemed like passages I had read before many times jumped out with new and inspiring meaning on a daily basis and God was speaking to me directly and personally. I could really say, "How sweet are your words to my taste, sweeter than honey to my mouth!"[4] But eventually, without warning and perhaps impacted by difficult circumstances, my QT would lapse into routine, something I did just for the sake of being able to say I did it. During the school year, it meant I had to wake up at least thirty minutes earlier, and when you're only sleeping three hours a night, those thirty minutes are costly.

3. Isa 55:8–9.
4. Ps 119:103.

As my passion waned, this feeling of empty ritual would also affect my other spiritual practices. I kept trying to make the right decisions and be faithful to my responsibilities, but with the excitement gone, it began to feel mechanical. Instead of performing these actions because I wanted to and out of love for God, I did them because I was supposed to. I regressed back into the legalistic religion God had drawn me out of. And I began to wonder why I tried so hard to live for God anyways.

Sometimes, I wished I could live in ignorance and not know what God thought about a situation. I mean, why did it matter that I cared about clothes? Did I really need to think that hard about it? It felt like God wouldn't let me get away with anything. Life was hard enough as it was, without having to examine my heart and nitpick at all the possible wrong in it. It just added another layer of anxiety to brood over. And did God really have my best interest at heart? Would everything really work out?

I blamed myself in turn, saying, "You don't trust God enough. You're not doing enough. You need to try harder." But at the same time, I questioned God repeatedly: "Where are you? Did I do something wrong? Is that why you've distanced yourself from me? God, I feel lonely/tired/anxious/sad. Why aren't you helping me? God, I'm tired of doing the right thing; is this worth it? God, do you even care?" During those times, it was hard to believe that God would never leave or forsake me.[5]

But in the end, these dry seasons were what grew me the most spiritually, just as an athlete grows stronger by pushing beyond conscious limits. I began to see God's purpose through the difficult circumstances and that God's word truly was trustworthy. Through something as unremarkable as clothes, God opened my eyes to see the things that mattered and, at the same time, taught me greater compassion.

If I didn't want people to judge me based on clothes, what right did I have to judge others based on what they wore? Sometimes, I would catch myself looking critically at someone's outfit and realize, "Wow, I am so hypocritical!" I wanted to look beyond the surface to see each person and love them the way God did. My desire to be liked for who I was beyond the clothes I wore taught me to treat and value people the same regardless of social stature or other superficial accoutrements.

It made me reflect upon what made one person "cool" and another person "uncool." Could someone wear brand-name clothing and automatically be popular? Or did they also have to be physically attractive? Was it their demeanor? Why was this person allowed to hang out with that group, while others were barred from entry? It all seemed so arbitrary. I watched

5. Heb 13:5.

during lunchtime when a classmate—definitely not in the cool zone—tried to hang out with the cool kids at their table. They were not blatantly mean to her, but their body language expressed that she was not welcome. Later I was told they used a nickname behind her back that was unquestionably mean. That made me sad. Why couldn't everyone be friends with anyone? Where did these invisible barriers come from?

I eventually perceived the unseen need and desire that all people have to be loved. There were those rare moments when masks would come down and I'd discover the very real pain that people were going through, the hurt they covered up at school with their persona. It appeared as if everyone put on a show in order to be loved and respected, hiding their flaws and pain. Those were the things that made them feel unworthy of love and seemed to create those invisible barriers. This was why everyone couldn't be friends with anyone. People were too busy protecting themselves. It brought to mind the image of Adam and Eve hiding from God and covering their nakedness and shame with fig leaves.[6]

This insight altered the kind of leader I wanted to be. Truthfully speaking, maybe these epiphanies wouldn't have mattered as much if I had been at the bottom of the social ladder. I would have just developed noble ideals without the ability or opportunity to apply them. The reality was that I *was* in a position of influence as an athlete and class officer, so much so that it might have surprised people to discover the insecurities I dealt with. However, as God worked in me and affirmed my value, these insecurities ultimately made me a better leader—one who didn't use my position to demean others to feel better about myself, but rather one who affirmed the value of others without prejudice. I understood that no matter which clique we were a part of or what clothes we wore, we were equals before God.

Who knew all that could come out of a struggle with wanting new clothes? Even though I still sometimes wished for better clothes, little by little I saw the truth of those verses come to life over time.

If I had been given all the possessions and the position I wanted, I could easily have continued to depend on surface characteristics to judge myself and others. I don't know that I would have ever stopped to even think about people outside the inner social circle. However, being only somewhat "in"—and uncomfortably so—helped me to see myself more clearly as God saw me (my flaws as well as my value). My character grew and, as a leader, I gained a new perspective to see the unseen.

My senior year, one of my friends told me, "Eunice, you are one of the most respected people in our class." As confirmation of that, to my surprise,

6. Gen 3:7–8.

I was voted by my class to be the female graduation speaker. I'm pretty sure I wasn't voted for because of my looks or stylish clothes. To me, this spoke instead to the value of being a person of integrity who treated everyone with respect and kindness, regardless of their social standing.

As for ending up at UW, it took years before faith became sight. It wasn't until I graduated that I began to fully see how wonderful my experience at UW had been and to be thankful to God for leading me there. My time at UW literally determined the course of my life. I met one of my dearest friends there, and the scholarship gave me the financial flexibility to study abroad in Korea, where I met my husband—not to mention the freedom that came from finishing school without debt.

From my high school vantage point, I could never have imagined all the ways I would grow—not only intellectually but also spiritually and personally—and the good that would come out of it. God could see years down the road, whereas I could only guess. In humility and repentance, I confessed that God's thoughts and ways were indeed higher than mine. God really did know better than me, and God's plans were for my good. Putting my faith in God had not been in vain because I discovered God was exactly who I had been told by God.

Now that almost two decades have passed since I finished high school, I can evaluate my inability to get into other colleges with greater objectivity. While my GPA was excellent, my SAT score and essays likely fell short of their standards. I don't say this with any self-deprecation but simply with less naiveté and better knowledge of what it takes to make it into the top universities. In that light, the scholarship was indeed an enormous gift of God's grace: tuition completely covered at the one school for which I was legitimately qualified.

Through these seasons of discipline, God paradoxically led me to greater freedom. While I knew what God said, I was often still caught in the old ways of judging myself and the world. It was difficult to believe in my own intrinsic value, but God's discipline made it real. I also became less dependent on circumstances and people, and surer of my identity and purpose. This left me free to think about myself less and more about others.

But the greatest fruit of these dry seasons was a deeper communion with God and learning the meaning of being satisfied by God alone. They made me thirstier and dug a deeper well within me so that I could be more satiated than ever before. I discovered that the drier the wood, the greater the blaze once kindled. The desert season, though painful at the time, was more than worth it because it eventually brought about a greater encounter with God than I had previously known. I experienced God again as a very real presence, passion reawoke in me, and I could pray like David, "Because your steadfast love is better than life, my lips will praise you. . . . My soul is satisfied as with a rich feast."[7]

God took me through these periods not to force obedience (again, discipline did not mean punishment) but simply to bring me to know God more deeply. This grew my faith, which, in turn, increased my desire and willingness to submit to God. When I witnessed God's promises come to life, I knew I could trust God's word. This process taught me that God's love was even greater than I had imagined. God's way was indeed worth it, not only because good things did eventually happen but mainly because it enabled me to encounter God.

There were moments when God's *presence* was with me in such a real way that it seemed like I could reach out and touch God's face with my hand. God's love felt like it surrounded me and satisfied a deep longing in my heart that nothing else could. In those moments when God felt so near, my heart overflowed with repentance and humility for my sin, as well as unspeakable joy, gratitude, and rest. There was nowhere else I would've rather been, and I wanted God more than anything else. This kind of communion and sense of completeness was worth self-denial and sacrifice.

God showed me that if I willingly yielded, God would lead me to an overflowing life and remove me from the traps of pride, fear, and shame. Everything else in life came and went; nothing human or circumstantial was fully reliable. But I didn't have to fear inevitable failures because God remained steadfast.

Lesson followed lesson until God brought me to a place during my junior year in college where once and for all I made a commitment to follow whatever God asked of me. I didn't want to compromise; I wanted to live in complete obedience the life God wanted for me. I committed to surrendering every area and decision of my life because I was convinced that wherever and however God took me was the best possible life.

---

7. Ps 63:3, 5.

4

The Perfect God

My spiritual discoveries brought me to an understanding of God as deeply personal and relational. Why did it matter to God whether I obeyed out of trust versus obligation? Because God was relational. My desire for intimate relationships of love and mutuality, for genuine connection with others, simply reflected God's own nature because I was created in God's image.

"Relational" didn't imply that God and I were somehow on the same footing. God was still infinitely great and did ask for obedience, but God didn't want to remain distant from me the way a master stands apart from his servant. Incredibly, God wanted me to know God as God already knew me—not just know *about*, but know in the most intimate and experiential way possible so that I obeyed and committed to God out of my own volition. This fundamentally transformed the concept of absolute submission to God. It made me more than a passive object that simply did what I was told. Rather, it acknowledged my independent identity and my agency as an active partner.

I realized that when God led me in directions I didn't want to go, it was safe to voice my feelings, just as David's psalms frequently vent his fear and distress. While obedience entailed no compromise, God didn't make unilateral decisions that disregarded my desires and feelings. Instead, God gave me space to express my thoughts and opinions. Similarly, when things didn't work out my way and I grew angry, I learned that God could handle my anger. God never punished me for being upset. The important thing was that I never stopped coming to God and that I maintained an open channel of communication, even in my "imperfect" emotions.

This interaction brought me closer to God because it gave me the opportunity not only to be heard, but also to hear God. Once I felt heard and understood, I was more open to God's voice and willing to submit, trusting that God would never betray me to my fears and anxieties. They were held safely in God's hands. The result was that over time, if I knew God was telling me to do something, I'd ultimately choose it—even through my griping—because my spirit couldn't rest otherwise. Paradoxically, even if it hurt in a way, being within God's will brought peace and gladness to my mind and heart.

Of course, in the end, God was always right. Time would inevitably show God's wisdom and trustworthy character. It was in my shortsightedness that I resisted what God wanted.

It was very much about the process. God allowed me to come to these conclusions on my own as I wrestled and searched for answers. God wanted to bring me into union without compromising the integrity of my own agency. Ultimately, if I came to see that God knew and loved me—and that God was completely good—how could I *not* follow willingly?

God's personal nature even made rebuke welcome. Being relational, God didn't want to diminish my identity but to fulfill it. God alone knew the potential created in me, and it was in submission to God that I could reach that potential.

According to Psalm 139 (yet another one of David's psalms), God knew me better than I knew myself.[1] God penetrated the innermost depths of my soul, into layers and crannies I didn't even know about, or maybe didn't *want* to know about (like repressed memories in psychology). I didn't want to look too closely at myself because I feared discovering evidence that would confirm the insecurity and low self-worth I felt. This would set in stone that my whole identity was indeed something to be ashamed of.

Having someone know you that intimately might sound scary—threatening even—but it actually brought the opposite to me: safety. God's intimate knowledge of me was underpinned by the truth of the cross, which had already established my ultimate identity as God's daughter, completely loved. No matter what, I was good enough. No matter what, I was still loved

---

1. "O Lord, you have searched me and known me. You know when I sit down and when I rise up; you discern my thoughts from far away. You search out my path and my lying down, and are acquainted with all my ways. Even before a word is on my tongue, O Lord, you know it completely. . . . Search me, O God, and know my heart; test me and know my thoughts. See if there is any wicked way in me, and lead me in the way everlasting" (Ps 139:1–4, 23–24).

and valued. No matter what discovery about me rose to the surface, nothing could subtract from that identity.

As a result, I could listen when God corrected me without feeling defensive. In fact, God was the only one with whom I could be completely real because God already knew everything I was thinking and feeling. There was no fear of disappointing because God already knew every shortcoming. Thus, I could bring my failures to God without fear of rejection or condemnation. God *already* knew. God also knew all my intentions (good and bad), so I took confidence in the fact that God would never misjudge me. God wanted me to come, so God could receive me in my frailty, forgive me, and give me the chance to start again.

And even when firm, God was also gentle in reproof. It always amazed me how God would speak to me so clearly and unmistakably—through a verse I encountered in my QT, then again in a book, and then again in a sermon at precisely the right moment. God consistently revealed God's thoughts about situations in my life, confirmed through several different sources, so that I couldn't miss it. It astounded me that God would traverse the space between God's celestial abode and the lowly sphere of earth, enter into the commonplace among billions of people, and penetrate through the haze of my clouded mind to speak just to *me*. When this happened, I never felt knocked down or crushed—deeply convicted, yes, but also moved that God cared enough to reach out to me.

But what made God's discipline most remarkable was that God didn't just tell me what I did wrong in order to simply modify my behavior. God revealed how my wrongdoings were often rooted in a misconception of God's character and in my identity as God's child. In this way, God's correction always reestablished my identity instead of undercutting it. It still hurt in the sense that it's hard to face yourself in complete honesty and see where you are wrong. But it was a cathartic pain that brought relief. I didn't have to carry the burden of guilt and shame anymore, and I could truly see a refining process taking place within my heart as I grew in humility, grace, patience, wisdom, and more.

Sometimes, I wondered why God even bothered with me. I felt like I just kept making the same mistakes, relearning the same lessons, and still doubting—even after all that God had done for me. Yet God was persistent and never gave up on me, patiently growing me little by little. I learned to welcome God's correction, hoping God would never stop being so personally involved in my life and keeping me close.

I couldn't help loving God because God was so perfect in every way toward me.

REFLECTION

1. How did your parents and other adults in your life teach you about God and model who God is?

2. How do you understand God? Is God someone to please in order to avoid punishment, or is God someone who allows you to engage with God? If you could sum up in one sentence or five adjectives how you understand God, what would it/they be?

3. What else might have influenced your understanding of God?

4. How has your understanding of God changed or been reinforced by your experiences?

5. Have you ever had an experience that challenged everything you thought you knew about God? How did you resolve it, if at all?

Part 2

Deconstruction

I stood on the sand gazing at the expansive ocean with its unceasing, rolling waves, the sun shining down on it toward the horizon as if inviting me to see something hidden beyond the course of normal everyday life. The wind whipped around me, a continuous reminder of the very real presence of things mysterious and unseen. The ocean had always been a reflection to me of the vastness yet intimate nearness of God. I hoped that in such a setting, God would enter into my desolation and speak.

"God," I prayed, "please let your word speak to me." A prayer I always prayed before reading my Bible. I hoped this time that maybe, just maybe, something I was about to read would bring a glimmer of understanding into my confusion.

I opened my Bible and began to read from the first chapter of Malachi. I had only read a few verses when I stopped in my tracks: "A son honors his father, and servants their master. If then I am a father, where is the honor due me? And if I am a master, where is the respect due me? says the Lord of hosts."[1] I was dumbfounded. God did speak, but in a way I had never expected. Through this verse, I heard God clearly say to me, "You honor your parents more than me."

I approached the job search furnished with my own theology, believing deeply in God's grace, the goodness of God's plan for me, God's trustworthiness,

---

1. Mal 1:6.

and God's relational nature. I had a willingness to do anything God asked me to do and a desire to do only what God wanted me to do.

It was with this foundation that I decided to take a break from the job search and seek God's leading in prayer. In my mind, it was based on a commitment to fully believing in who God had always shown Godself to be over my own fears and emotions, and radically living 100 percent according to how God led me.

I knew that what I was doing made absolutely no sense and that I was truly being foolish if it wasn't God telling me to stand my ground and wait on God's direction. I wanted to believe that the same God of the Bible still lived, acted, and spoke today. If God didn't, then I was just imagining things, and there was no reason to deviate from the standard job-search process.

But if God *was* real, if God *was* the God of Abraham and Moses, who raised Jesus from the dead, then I could live according to God's word rather than human calculation. The promises I held onto were that God would lead me if I trusted in God and not in my own understanding;[2] that if I sought God, I would find God;[3] that if I persistently went to God in prayer, God would answer me;[4] that if I waited on God, God would bring things about in God's time; and that if I sought God's kingdom first, all my necessities would be taken care of.[5] Therefore, I didn't need to follow convention. I could trust God to do only what God could do.

From my perspective, this was a critical juncture of my life—as important as a life-defining decision to strike out for an unknown land—and the culmination of all I had learned about living by faith. I'm not saying that everyone should follow this path. But given my particular struggles and everything I had learned spiritually up to this point, I believed this was being faithful to what God had taught me.

However, as my parents pushed back, the stakes intensified. It turned into a battle between their belief system and mine. In my mind, my parents were expecting me to submit mechanically to their authority and cultural norms; in other words, to revert back to the religion of obligation and appearances that I had evolved out of. On my part, I was betting everything on the belief that God was first and foremost relational and allowed—even encouraged—me to engage with God. That God was a higher authority than my parents. This raised the crucial question: was God a freeing, benevolent king or a domineering dictator?

---

2. Prov 3:5–6.

3. Jer 29:13.

4. Matt 7:7; Luke 11:9.

5. Matt 6:25–33; Luke 12:22–31.

As the pressure mounted, it seemed less and less valid to trust my own understanding of God. Even though I felt like God was saying to stand my ground and continue waiting on God's direction, I couldn't be confident in what I thought. Ultimately, I consciously chose to subordinate my own belief system and superimposed on it an opposing worldview I disagreed with.

It's not that I had never had to alter my belief system before, but those previous adjustments had come as a result of careful reflection and conviction. This was different. It was as if I looked at a blue ball *knowing* it was blue, but because my parents and society told me it was red, I knowingly lied to myself and forced myself to believe it was red. My personal autonomy had been completely compromised.

Then, when a job opportunity suddenly came the next day and everything fell into place, it was as if God approved. It seemed as though the job opportunity came *because* I gave in to my parents, like I was being rewarded for my obedience to them. After all, didn't the Bible also command me to honor and obey my parents? So wasn't it reasonable to conclude I did the right thing in submitting to them, especially considering the ensuing outcome?

However, this threw everything I had learned about God into profound confusion. At face value, it appeared as if my parents had been right in their philosophy and I had been wrong in mine; they had won. Gone was the God who invited personal autonomy. Faith didn't involve an interpersonal relationship but was only about unilateral obedience after all—both to God and also my parents; and I was nothing. This is what left me so desolate. The chair had been pulled out from under me in the most important relationship in my life, by the person I trusted more than anyone else.

What hurt even more was that I had been waiting for God to simply tell me I was wrong, if indeed I was wrong. If God had done so and let me choose to obey as God had always done in the past, it would've resulted in the same job outcome while still maintaining my autonomy. But instead, it felt as if God had smacked me down and then ground my face into the mud to show me I was wrong. Why did I need to be treated so harshly if I had developed a trusting relationship and was willing to be corrected? Had the relationship just been a mirage?

In the weeks that followed, as I adjusted to my new work life and the dust settled around me, I attempted to pick up the pieces. I considered my previous encounters with God and Scripture, and chose to believe they were real. I admitted that they didn't witness to this tyrannical God. I began to try to process everything in order to understand the why behind the events. Where was God in all of this, and could God be trying to teach me something? I had often found, upon exiting a crisis in my life, that I could look

back and see a new lesson—an explanation showing, contrary to appearances, that God was still loving and good. I had simply been unable to see
the larger picture. Maybe, I thought, I was missing a perspective here.

For this reason, I sought a way to make sense of how things had un-
folded. I looked for a purpose that aligned more consistently with who God
had previously shown Godself to be.

First, I considered the possibility that while I thought I was willing to
be wrong, God knew it would take more to open my eyes. So maybe God
allowed me to give in to my parents so that I would actually say yes when
the opportunity came. Perhaps I was more stubborn than I realized. But this
explanation didn't satisfy me. The ends did not justify the means, and God
had shown me repeatedly the importance of process over results.

I next entertained the idea that I hadn't been wrong to approach the
job search the way I did but was wrong in yielding to my parents' pressure.
The job opportunity was coming anyway, and if I had held out one more day,
I would have been validated. I would've seen God work things out just as I
had trusted God would.

But even that didn't help because I turned it back to God again. The
fact was that it didn't work out that way, and I *had* succumbed to my parents'
pressure. If I hadn't been wrong, then why didn't God give me the strength
to persevere; where was the transcendent peace that would give me the
wings to soar above the fray? What happened to promises like "I can do all
things through [Christ] who strengthens me"[6] and "those who wait for the
Lord shall renew their strength"?[7] Why didn't God help me to hold on? Just
one more day. I thought that as long as I knew God wanted me to do something, I would do it, and God would help me do it. But instead, I had felt
alone, abandoned by God to face an insurmountable challenge on my own.

Either direction I went, questions remained. God didn't seem to be
the God I had come to trust. I kept moving in circles and hitting a wall
because no matter how I pondered the event, the fact remained that my
personal autonomy had been compromised. Why had God allowed that if
God indeed was relational and valued my autonomy? To justify myself was
to undermine God, but to justify God was to undermine myself—the self
that God had shaped and grown these past years.

A step toward enlightenment took place on that beach when God
spoke clearly and rebuked me in unmistakable terms for allowing my parents' word to supersede God's. God held me responsible for a choice I had

6. Phil 4:13.

7. Isa 40:31.

made, even while I was questioning why *God* had allowed such a thing. *I had done it. Not God.*

I hadn't seen it as a choice at all.

And that alone was deeply telling.

How did this happen when I had believed myself to be fully committed to God above all else? I thought I had unmistakably distinguished my own theology from my parents' and even viewed their ministry with a critical eye. In many ways, my faith had become a way to preserve my independence apart from the expectations of my parents and other adults at church—a validation and refuge for my own thoughts and identity. And yet, clearly, my parents' authority still held so much power over me that I chose to listen to them over God. It was as if two different warring factions wrestled within me. I had thought one was appropriately subdued, but like a clandestine investor surreptitiously acquiring a majority stake for a hostile takeover, it suddenly rose up and subdued *me*.

Apparently, I still had so much to uncover among the unmined realities of how I understood my identity.

5

A House Divided

As I've recounted, my high school and college years brought about exciting revelations and intimacy with God. Unfortunately, learning about God as a relational, intimate God brought my relationship with my parents under scrutiny. One might assume that because I was growing in faith, I should also have been growing closer to my parents due to our "shared" beliefs. But in reality, it caused a lot of tension.

My parents contributed to my struggles with perfectionism, pressure to perform, and image consciousness. In many ways, they represented the very ideas that God was teaching me to let go of. Thus, even though my parents were devout Christians, I often sought refuge in God from their criticism, lack of understanding, and what I considered unreasonable discipline.

My spiritual values began to resist their cultural values. There was already a gap by virtue of the fact that my parents emigrated from Korea as adults, while I was born in the US. As children, my siblings and I lost much of our Korean language ability after we started school and adopted English as our primary language. My dad's attempt to preserve our roots by restricting us to speaking only Korean at the dinner table simply led to the cessation of conversation and a deafening silence. Every day, I performed a balancing act between trying to be American enough to fit in at school and trying to be Korean enough for my parents and the church adults. But over time, my Americanized sensibilities began to take precedence.

Korean households are built on filial piety and a commitment to the collective good. To maintain these values, they stress obedience to authority, respect for one's elders, fulfilling one's duty, and correction. Absent were concepts like sharing emotions and positive reinforcement. Furthermore, Korean immigrant parents show their love through providing—often at great sacrifice—and through disciplinary action. The main objective was to provide a foundation by which their children could establish financial security in their future. However, this led to an emphasis on achievements and less focus on intangibles, like encouragement, affection, and personal presence. Many second-generation Korean American children would agree that their parents went to great lengths to give them opportunities, such as better education or music lessons, but were lacking in emotional support—something that growing up in America taught me to long for.

In a culture where the individual reigns, I learned to believe that my own identity and emotions mattered and should be considered. The influence of American media and entertainment, in particular, drove a deeper wedge between my parents and me. How many TV shows and movies featured an adolescent pursuing a journey of self-discovery, finding out that she must be "true to herself" in order to be genuinely happy? That she can't just do what her parents want but that personal happiness matters just as much? *Dirty Dancing, Titanic,* and *She's the Man,* just to name a few. Disney—that monolith forming and projecting American values—loves this theme, and its female leads often depict this struggle: Ariel from *Little Mermaid,* Jasmine from *Aladdin,* and even an Asian version in *Mulan.*

Watching American sitcoms like *Full House* and *Boy Meets World* conveyed idyllic family dynamics. Even when the kids made choices their parents disapproved of, they were given the opportunity to tell their side of the story. Parents taught in such a way that the kids understood what they did wrong. When something troubled them at school or in relationships, their parents were often there to provide sage advice and comfort.

Then I had the living examples of my white friends and their seemingly easygoing lives. Besides sleepovers and rewards for grades, they regularly slept in on weekends, invited each other to their houses, and went to birthday parties. Their parents also supported them emotionally and socially by participating in non-school activities, like cheering them on at sports games, bringing cupcakes for birthdays, and giving rides to various gatherings.

I loved my parents and wanted to please them, but these cultural influences and my developing selfhood rebelled more and more against their (from my perspective) autocratic ways. My parents' expectations frustrated me because they seemed to focus only on what I did outwardly, without really knowing what I was going through inwardly. Only *they* could be right. And their constant correction, without positive affirmation, made me feel misunderstood and unable to do anything right. No matter how hard I tried in school or church, only my shortcomings were seen. My strengths were never mentioned, and perhaps more importantly, the fact that I tried my best wasn't recognized. Effort and intentions were meaningless; the only thing of value seemed to be performance.

For instance, despite working hard to earn a 4.0 every semester in high school without even being told to do so, I never heard from my mom until the one time I brought home a progress report with an A- and a B+ during my senior year. This instantly triggered me. How hard I tried, how stressed I was, how little sleep I got, how much character I built—nothing but the results seemed to matter. Just as long as I continued to appear perfect outwardly, they were happy—regardless of whether I was happy.

I got defensive with my mom for only pointing out the two "imperfect" grades, asking why she had to focus exclusively on those. She, in turn, brought up my SAT scores. Angrily, she compared me with my cousin, who had come from Korea only three years prior and studied so hard for his SATs that he got a better score on his verbal section than me. She said, "Aren't you embarrassed that your cousin, whose first language isn't even English, scored better than you?"

At that point, my anger boiled over, and I left the house crying, slamming the front door in fury behind me. I just had to get away. To be compared with my cousin on our SATs made me feel like my mom overlooked everything else I did, including the fact that I was in a much more rigorous academic program and had maintained a 4.0 most semesters at my own independent direction. No matter what I achieved, there was always some other benchmark I had failed to reach, some other way in which I was lacking. I was exhausted, and it frustrated me not only that my parents focused on outward appearances but also that I felt the need to stifle my own identity in order to meet their standards.

You might dismiss this as typical teenage angst, but my experience with God's relational nature had shown me a concept of discipline that was completely different from what my parents demonstrated. This elevated my conflict with my parents from simply cultural to spiritual. I could never deny that my parents loved me and sincerely wanted what was best for me, but did they *know* me? I definitely didn't feel known by them, and if they didn't really know me, then how could I believe they knew what was best for me? If they didn't really know me, then how could I not feel like they were only forcing me to do what they wanted? In truth, I probably should've invested more time studying for the SATs given my ardent desire to study out of state. But when my mom criticized me about this, it felt like it was more for her than for me.

As they continued to insist on their own way without making space for my feelings or perspective, this relationship with my parents forced me into the role of a passive object—which was problematic even when they were right. The relationship felt entirely one-sided. I could try to make my parents happy while suppressing my own desires and beliefs, but their constant criticism of my shortcomings would inevitably leave me feeling frustrated, inadequate, and defensive. Was it worth the expense of my identity?

In total contrast, my relationship with God was teaching me that I wasn't a mere passive player. God knew me, my thoughts and opinions mattered, and I believed my power to choose should be respected. To love but not know wasn't enough.

This dynamic was reinforced at a macro-level in my Korean American church. There, the interaction between the first- and second-generation Korean congregants mirrored my struggle with my parents' preoccupation with image and fear that they were swallowing up my identity.

It began with the formation of a church within the church, one that spoke English instead of Korean. The church created a separate service for the American-born children to allow for age-appropriate education in a language they understood better. Then, as the children grew older, a separate English-language youth service similarly became necessary.

By the time we became old enough to join the main "adult" service, integration was no longer an option. During the time we had our own children's and youth services, not only was the language different, but our entire structure and philosophy of spiritual expression had diverged. As a result, the separate English Ministry (EM) developed, composed mainly of second-generation Korean Americans and heavily influenced by American Evangelicalism—an alternative to what became known as the Korean Ministry (KM).

Overall, the KM's way of worship was much more ritualistic than that of the EM. Services followed a traditional Presbyterian structure of hymns and liturgy (standing and sitting at preordained moments and reciting the Apostle's Creed and the Lord's Prayer, for example). It was highly formal, as opposed to the simpler structure and contemporary songs of our EM service, which seemed to allow for more expressive and sincere worship. The KM also assessed devotion by consistent attendance at Sunday services, early morning weekday prayer services, Wednesday night service, and other church events.

Perhaps the KM's traditionalism and unyielding commitment to the point of exhaustion and poor health wouldn't have turned me off so much had this apparent piety coincided with transformation of character and spiritual growth. But the dissonance between their outward commitment to church activities and their personal behavior ultimately made me view their worship as all for show and therefore legalistic.

It's not that I didn't care for the KM at all or had zero positive interactions with them. Just as I loved and appreciated my parents regardless of my frustrations, I held great affection for the KM members as well, despite my criticisms. I have wonderful memories of Memorial Day picnics eating grilled *galbi* (Korean short ribs) and playing games like dodgeball together. They also showed their affection for the youth and EM by generously supporting us with their time and finances (among other things) by attending and donating large sums at our fundraisers and letting us wash their cars even though we left them more smudged. When we played in church sports tournaments, they cooked delicious food for us, packed coolers full of Gatorade, and enthusiastically cheered us on with empty plastic water bottles filled with rocks. Two deaconesses, in particular, never forgot my siblings and me. Every year after the Christmas service, they would furtively beckon one of us to their cars, open the trunk, and hand us bags full of gifts. When I was lonely during my time in Honduras, the knowledge that a handful of KM women gathered and fervently prayed for me on a weekly basis comforted me. I felt the KM's concern, kindness, and care for us through these actions. They were family.

However, as a PK, I often received an inside glimpse into the politics and petty squabbles among the adults at church. It showed me how saving face mattered more than humble repentance. Direct confrontation was avoided for fear of offending someone, and yet grievances were liberally canvassed behind closed doors. People seemed unaware of or unwilling to acknowledge their misdeeds and pride. When I heard my parents discussing yet another conflict or how someone was upset with my dad for doing such and such was threatening to leave the church, it seemed like so much of the dissension was based on misunderstanding. It didn't surprise me that this lack of direct communication bred distrust and left ample room for misunderstanding to grow like a parasitic infection.

I asked my mom why they couldn't go directly to the person and just explain to them what really happened. She responded that it was cultural. However, it scared me when the same people who were upset with my parents or in conflict with other church members would smile and act deferentially toward my parents. To me, this wasn't a cultural problem; it was a blatant character problem, completely contrary to the kind of humility, patience, forgiveness, repentance, and openness that the church is called to. It brought to my mind Jesus's critique of the Pharisees for "[cleaning] the outside of the cup and of the plate, but inside [being] full of greed and self-indulgence."[1]

And so people continued to behave as if nothing was wrong, and problems were swept under the rug until they reached a crisis point. Then the next thing we knew, the church was thrown into turmoil and torn apart. One faction, having recruited supporters to their side (again, behind closed doors), departed in fury and self-righteousness, while the remaining members nursed their wounds in equally self-righteous belief.

This process exasperated (and grieved) me and made me further question the maturity of the adults' faith. How could people who claimed to love the same God and be filled with the same Spirit ever come to that point?[2] Wasn't the church supposed to be a united body? Wasn't division contrary to what Christ stood for? I couldn't comprehend how people who were so kind at times could fight with such bitterness, and it hurt to say goodbye to close friends whose parents decided to leave our church.

It frustrated me to see my dad's hands tied because of certain influential groups within the church who questioned his motives. They seemed to focus more on appearances than the infinitely more important matter of inner spiritual formation. For the adults, church was like a political playground, a space to exercise power and portray an image that would impress others.

Being born in the US, it was easy to villainize Korean culture. The first generation's fixation on image was confirmed to me through their desire to drive luxury cars, own designer handbags, and "humblebrag" about their children's accomplishments—which college they got into, what job they obtained, the gifts they bought, or the house they lived in. This all seemed to reflect the shallowness of their faith. Having chafed under their watchful, judgmental eyes my whole life, I found it difficult to respect their spiritual standing or relational dynamics, especially when they seemed to insist on wielding an authority that, in my opinion, they didn't deserve.

The way we (the EM) lived our faith, on the other hand, seemed to more accurately represent the love and grace that should characterize Christianity. There seemed to be more authentic responses and personal connection in our experience of God through music, fellowship, and retreats, as well as our disciplines of Bible reading, prayer, and serving others. More importantly, what we learned in worship and Bible study crossed over to our lives because we were actually changing. We were growing in character, integrity,

1. Matt 23:25; Luke 11:39.

2. My youthful idealism shows up here, as even Paul and Barnabas argued and went their separate ways (Acts 15:36–41).

our love for God, and leadership. In my (obviously humble, nonjudgmental, and objective) opinion at the time, the EM's spiritual disciplines, unlike the KM's, were rooted in the more important idea of being, as opposed to just doing. Our outward actions were linked to the inner life. We didn't do them just to look good; they led to real transformation.

When I saw the KM embroiled in yet another political conflict, I would look around at my close-knit EM, shake my head, and think, "This is what church is supposed to be like. Our relationships are so genuine; we'd never fight like that." We happily distanced ourselves from the fray, content to run our ministry as independently from the KM as possible.

However, even though we had our own worship service as young adults, we could never shake the second-class citizen feeling. No matter how old we got, we were always "the kids" and the KM members were "the adults," and our ministry didn't receive the same respect. It was as if we were playing church to them.

When we used the fellowship hall for services, the KM women in the kitchen would talk loudly, their voices disrupting the sanctity of our worship. When we changed our service time and began using the main worship hall, KM members would sometimes walk in during the middle of the service to put an item away in the pastoral office. And when the KM planned an activity, the EM was expected to participate—always on the KM's terms. When the KM asked the EM to do something, we were supposed to automatically say yes, regardless of our schedule or opinion on the matter. If we so much as hinted at the possibility of having other plans, we were rebuked as uncooperative. To us, their belittlement validated all of our critical attitudes toward them. It pushed us in the opposite direction, fueling a desire to separate ourselves so that we could be free.

As a result, by the time I graduated from college, I believed I had developed my own personal spiritual identity with a good working philosophy on how my faith should inform the way I lived. It was not only distinct from my parents' spiritual paradigm, but in all honesty, I thought it superior as well.

It's little wonder that my parents dismissed me, and I them, for not understanding where the other was coming from. Yet when our respective perspectives eventually met in a head-on collision, I rebounded back to my former belief—that the only valid option was to submit unquestioningly—with a force that left me bewildered and broken.

6

Introducing Enmeshment

AFTER WORKING IN MY job for two years, I decided to pursue a Master of Divinity (MDiv) degree at Fuller Theological Seminary. My time there was another incredible season of personal and spiritual growth. I wish every Christian, including laypeople, could attend seminary because of how it expands one's capacity to understand God, one's self, and the world. While this might make some uncomfortable, one of the roles seminary plays is to deconstruct and dissect how we think about God in order to deepen and broaden our understanding of God.

It would be impossible to compress and summarize four years of theological, biblical, and ministerial education into one or two chapters of a book about a personal spiritual journey. While every class contributed something to the ultimate synthesis of my formation, one of the most significant classes I took was Family Therapy and Pastoral Counseling, taught by Dr. David Augsburger.

This class guided me to see myself as part of a larger system, showing me how I unwittingly played out roles that I thought were expected of me and then depended on those roles to give me value. These roles, which were in many instances unscriptural, were also often unhealthy both for me and the system as a whole. This new lens gave me even further insight into understanding the conflict with my parents and set me on a path to finally finding resolution and healing.

A CRASH COURSE ON FAMILY SYSTEMS THERAPY

Most (if not all) families deal with some form of dysfunction—perhaps a spoiled child, a workaholic spouse, or the inability to make basic decisions (like where to eat dinner) without getting into a fight. There is often a narrative that the family subscribes to in these situations to explain the dysfunction, which tends to lay blame on an individual: "Our child acts out even though we try to discipline him," "We have marital problems because my wife works too much," or "If Dad would just tell us where he wants to eat instead of saying, 'Anywhere is fine,' we wouldn't argue!"

In response to this, family systems theory is built on the premise that the source of tension within families does not lie with a single member. Instead, there is a deeper underlying problem in how the family functions as a system, or complex organism, to manage stress.

It's as if stress follows the principle of the conservation of mass when it isn't dealt with directly. Emotional strain—such as anxiety, guilt, shame, grief, fear, or trauma—has an almost physical presence that can get passed like a ball from one person to another. It might change appearance or expression, but it comes from the same place. It won't stay hidden or repressed but must have an outlet somewhere, whether through dysfunctional behavior (such as addiction or isolation) or an actual psychological disorder.

Many of these stressors, if not resolved, become patterns that get passed on from generation to generation. They can be communicated implicitly, and any given stressor can be absorbed by the next generation simply because the prior generation has not healed. Even family secrets never remain truly secret because the emotional repercussions will unconsciously dictate the family's behavior, even if the source is not outwardly expressed.

A fictional example is a man (let's call him Norman) whose older brother stole his parents' money, ran away from home, and ended up dying on the streets. The parents' response is to never talk about his brother and act as if he never existed. The memory is too painful, their regrets and sense of failure too overpowering. His photos are removed from the walls and his room is kept locked up. But in trying to avoid their overwhelming grief and guilt, the parents do not realize that their unspoken emotional distress seeps into their relationship with Norman so that he carries a vague sense of shame. As a result, Norman goes from being a bright kid to a gloomy, withdrawn teenager who spends most of his time alone in his room.

The parents can't understand why Norman has changed so much. They explain it by saying he is lazy and antisocial. Plus, they say, the adolescent years are awkward anyways. They don't consider looking deeper at the family secret of their other son because doing so would force them to deal with their intense emotions—emotions that feel too excruciating and big to handle. It is easier to focus on Norman as the problem.

Since Norman never had the space to express and resolve this feeling of shame (and to discover this shame wasn't his to begin with), he carries it as an adult into his marriage and family. It becomes the ubiquitous undercurrent to his words and actions toward his children, who don't even know about their deceased uncle. In turn, this seed is implanted in his children.

The oldest daughter deals with this hidden shame by becoming an overachiever and surrounding herself with friends, believing that accomplishments and popularity can cover her fear of inadequacy. All the while, she has no inkling that this sense of shame has unwittingly been transferred through generations as a result of her grandparents' failure to address the tragedy of her uncle. It's also worth noting that while Norman and his daughter followed drastically different paths to expressing shame during their teenage years (dark and isolated versus lively and social), the root source was the same.

A large part of why this type of stress is not addressed directly and, as a result, manifests in unrecognizable ways is due to a concept called enmeshment. In an enmeshed family system, the whole is more important than the individuals. Members sacrifice their own needs, desires, and self in order to meet the emotional needs of the family to maintain a state of homeostasis. In other words, a person's individual identity does not exist apart from the family and is minor relative to the collective identity of the family. The result is a small sense of self.

Because dealing with the true source of tension threatens the family's equilibrium, the family unit absorbs the stress and develops a system to manage it. Individuals develop a pseudo-self—while suppressing their authentic self—in order to play the part the family needs. In Norman's example, he shares a subconscious agreement with his parents to internalize the darkness of their history and act as a "problem child," which enables them to avoid confronting their own painful emotions and to keep his brother a secret.

When a child misbehaves, there are many possibilities for the true tension his actions may conceal. One is that the father coddles his son because his wife intimidates him, and this provides an indirect way to feel in control. Perhaps his own mother exercised a strong, controlling arm, making him feel weak and easily intimidated. The wife may compound this dynamic by constantly pushing her husband to seek a job promotion, though her motivation comes from having seen her father repeatedly passed over at work and subsequently become depressed, distant, and alcohol-dependent.

This tension between husband and wife, driven by a mutual fear and desperation to avoid childhood experiences, is then displaced onto their son—the real source of his behavioral issues. The son is tacitly encouraged, even as his mother outwardly laments his spoiled nature, to continue this behavior. Playing the part of his pseudo-self—the spoiled child—enables his parents to avoid confronting their deeper internal struggles, as well as their disappointments with each other. As a result, the son has no opportunity to develop his own sense of self because his identity is co-opted by the need to harmonize his parents' inherited dysfunction.

It is commonly understood that oldest, middle, and youngest children often carry similar characteristics across families. These roles, however, often arise out of a need for different family members to take on various functions to maintain the enmeshed family's balance. Oldest children are often responsible, middle children are mediators or neglected, and the youngest are the most laid-back and used to being taken care of.

While some of these roles are natural, they can nevertheless carry deeper and damaging implications. Oldest children, in bearing the brunt of responsibility, can end up sacrificing their natural needs and desires as children in order to act as surrogate parents to younger siblings, especially in single or absentee-parent homes. Sometimes, a child may take the role of a scapegoat on whom all the family's problems are blamed. Alternately, a golden child might bear the hopes of the entire family and struggle under the heavy weight of the pressure to perform. In each scenario, a family member's identity rests on his or her allotted role and the needs of the family. Not bearing out that role can lead to guilt, shame, and confusion.

Another way of thinking about enmeshment is loyalty. This might be difficult to wrap one's mind around because loyalty is typically viewed as a virtue. But the critical question is: Loyalty to what? In this form, loyalty shapes decisions at the cost of one's true identity and emotional health. Enmeshment can produce a family loyalty that defends the status quo although it is restrictive or even abusive.

Messages like "That's just how we've always done it" or "All the Lees love camping" implicitly convey that disagreement equals disloyalty. They can even carry a veiled threat: fall in line or else—or else the family will fall apart and it will be your fault; or else you will be rejected by the family; or else Mom and Dad will be devastatingly unhappy. This creates a compelling pressure to conform to collective family beliefs even against one's personal needs or desires. While these examples might seem innocuous, family "loyalty" can be a slippery slope that, at its extreme, can even cause a child to conceal child abuse or other terrible crimes that take place behind closed doors.

Have you ever wondered why it's so hard for you to agree with your parents or spouse outwardly even if you agree with them in your mind? I would wager that enmeshment has a large part to do with it—that your self is resisting being swallowed up completely by the system's identity and expectations for you, trying to carve out and protect a little morsel of self that still belongs to you.

Finally, enmeshment often intensifies in unstable families, such as those in frequent transition or experiencing trauma. This can take many forms, including immigration to a new country, repeated moving, or financial volatility. In such cases, familiarity and togetherness offer a stability that is important for survival, and personal desires must be even more readily sacrificed to protect the collective family unit from an unpredictable outside world.[1]

My family therapy class with Dr. Augsburger blew my mind and made the four years completing my MDiv degree worth it. The insights I gained allowed me to see my family under a new framework and to assess how it functioned as an enmeshed system. This helped unlock the mystery of why I had allowed myself to compromise my autonomy during my job search. Once I understood how deeply enmeshed I was with my parents, everything made more sense. Enmeshment explained the vague, recurring thoughts and fears that had flitted in and out of my mind throughout my life.

I began to view my perfectionist drive through the lens of my family role and how that role shaped my paradigm of reality. In a tension-filled family, I took upon myself the responsibility of being the happy one and cheering up the rest of the family. To do this, I sought to constantly regulate the emotional temperature of my family: I kissed my mom if she was in a bad mood, hugged my dad if he was upset, and listened to my brother vent if he was angry. When I couldn't do anything physically to help, I simply felt bad for the person, like my sister if she got in trouble (as if feeling bad would somehow take some of the stress from her).

I also pressured myself to succeed in the most quantifiable ways because as the youngest of immigrant parents, I thought I had to make the most of the advantages I had been given. Compared to my older sisters, I got to participate in more activities, and we were more settled financially while I was growing up. My oldest sister especially lived an exemplary life: she had navigated secondary school, gotten into college, paid her own way through, found a stable career, and earned her master's; and she had to figure out much of it on her own because my parents were unfamiliar with the American system. She had no model to follow. I, on the other hand, had her to help me with my homework. I also had three siblings paving the way before me. I believed my successes were their successes: I would be the golden child and sister, ensuring that their efforts propelled me to even higher heights.

---

1. To learn more about family systems therapy, see the Appendix for resources.

Although I knew at some level that I was unduly motivated by others' expectations, I was completely unaware of how deeply I had internalized my parents' emotions in particular. My identity depended on meeting what I perceived as their emotional needs. I believed my job in life and in the family—my purpose—was to bring them happiness, ease their stress, and redeem the physical exertions and financial sacrifices they made on my behalf. Doing so made me feel valuable.

Being perfect was a way of over-functioning so as not to add any more strain to my parents, as well as to give them something to be happy about. I preferred to take on more stress if I could somehow relieve my parents of some of their stress. I had thought my drive for a 4.0 GPA was self-motivated, but in reality, it was to fulfill what I saw as my role in the family. My parents never needed to tell me directly I had to get straight As. I had seen their pleasure and pride at my sister's valedictorian status—and their disappointment in my second sister's academic struggles. Their approval mattered, but their happiness mattered the most. Every positive or negative word, glance, or gesture spoke to their happiness or unhappiness, and I built my life accordingly.

Up until I graduated from college, regardless of what I told myself about why I strove so unbendingly for excellence ("It's all for God's glory" and "It's only right that I try so hard because then I can faithfully reflect the gifts God has given me"), the truth was that I was still exhibiting the model life of a Korean American daughter for the most part. Sure, my parents and I had our fights, but I was essentially doing what they wanted (earning good grades and going to church, and while my parents would have preferred that I study more for my SATs, a full-ride scholarship gave them something to be proud of) even as my inward views diverged from theirs. The visible results thus conveniently glossed over any underlying conflict. For the time being, I was able to have my cake and eat it too: I kept my inner, personal autonomy while appeasing my parents' desires.

But the job search brought an unavoidable collision between belief and action. It was no longer possible for both sides to be satisfied with the same outcome. And in that critical moment, while I didn't have the tools and language to understand it then, my struggle and ultimate decision betrayed how enmeshed I was with my parents.

I now realized that what tore me up the most during this conflict was how they questioned my motives and reproached me as if I didn't care at all about how my choices affected them because this was fundamentally contrary to how I had lived the past twenty-two years. The reality was that I cared intensely. I cared to the point that I had tried so hard to be so good for *their* sakes, to bring good into their lives and to compensate for their stress, losses, and sorrows. Despite this, my disagreement on one decision instantly rendered me a selfish, lazy daughter in their eyes. It reminded me of the A- and B+ I had received on my progress report—all the other perfect grades didn't matter. No matter how hard I worked to take away some of the burden from my parents' difficult lives and make them happy, they didn't seem to see any of it. But I desperately needed them to see it in order to feel okay with myself; I needed them to see that I wasn't casually abandoning my familial role or callously disregarding them. My attempts to reason with my mom and explain myself were efforts to get her to see precisely that.

As long as my parents were at odds with me, I couldn't be fully confident that I was doing the right thing. I was only good if I made them happy and altogether bad if they were anything but. And therein lay the rub: to do something they were unhappy about, I needed my parents to be happy with it. It was a catch-22. I could tell myself over and over that I only needed God's approval, but the truth was that my parents' emotional state defined me. As a result, I endlessly examined and reexamined my motives, ping-ponging between what I thought God wanted and my parents' displeasure. Guided by this core, unconscious operating system, I was defeated before I even began.

7

False Narratives

BUT THERE WAS MORE. Dr. Augsburger explained how the family system didn't operate in a vacuum but coexisted with and was influenced by other systems. When he described how churches could also be enmeshed, a spark went off in my brain. I knew immediately that my family wasn't only an enmeshed unit within itself but was also deeply enmeshed with the church in which I grew up.

The class began to break down for me the layers upon layers of various narratives that reinforced the idea that my identity depended on my parents' happiness. My family was a part of not just any church, but specifically a Korean church. And not just any Korean church, but one located in the US that was composed of immigrant families.

In a way, I dwelt in the center of concentric circles, with my "self" in the center, surrounded by the immediate circle of my family, which was surrounded by the church, which existed within Korean culture, which possessed its own distinct immigrant permutation. Each of these circles intertwined with one another and reached inward to shape my sense of self. And unfortunately, they all reinforced the idea that my parents' emotions defined who I was.

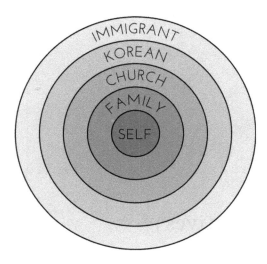

I've already addressed the family circle in the previous chapter. Taking the next circle, the enmeshment of my family with the church meant that I carried the aggregate weight of the church's expectations in addition to those of my parents.

The reality was that I didn't particularly care what church members thought of me as an individual. Rather, what really mattered was how their view of me reflected upon my parents. I wanted to shield my parents from criticism and give them something to be proud of in front of church members in order to bolster the respect church members showed them. I believed my parents needed me to behave as a proper daughter to save face in front of the church members they served as spiritual authorities. While my parents never complimented me at home, I would indirectly hear praise from church members based on stories my parents told them of my various accomplishments. Or I would hear church members compliment me to my parents while my parents smiled modestly, not wanting to gloat but with pleasure radiating from their faces. When this happened, this assured me that I was successfully fulfilling my role.

However, during my job search, when my mom used the church members' criticism to rebuke me, it signaled to me that I was now doing the opposite. It hurt that my mom would take to the opinions of church members over mine to judge me, and this confirmed to me that my mom's happiness was linked to what they thought. I feared how my actions made her look to them and how my apparent straying from the straight and narrow might jeopardize her standing as a mother and pastor's wife. It was one thing to make my mom unhappy, but the thought that I was also embarrassing her in front of our church members dramatically escalated the consequences of my actions.

Zooming out to the next layer, Dr. Augsburger gave me a broader perspective on how different cultures can function as macro-enmeshed systems, applying pressure to behave according to socially acceptable norms and values. Specifically, he laid out the different ways that individualistic versus "sociocentric"[1] cultures define a healthy identity.

As you might guess, in an individualistic culture—like the US—the individual reigns supreme as an independent entity. Health and stability derive from a person's ability to make their own decisions and live apart from the influence of others. The right to do what is best for oneself is intrinsic.

Conversely, in a sociocentric culture, like Korea, an individual's identity depends on their place within the group; conformity and submission to authority are expected. Before acting, it is necessary to consider how a decision will affect other group members. Health and stability in this context therefore come from taking on expected communal responsibilities and complying with established rules. Viewed through this lens, it was normal and right for church members to judge the pastor and his family in order to urge compliance with the group's expectations.

I reflected upon how hierarchy and deference to authority—built into the language itself—were critical features of Korean culture. Various Korean social systems are built upon the structure of *hoobae* (junior) and *seonbae* (senior), including school, the workplace, and the military. Those who are younger or lower in rank must treat elders and superiors with absolute respect and address them using honorific speech. The *seonbae* can ask the *hoobae* to do virtually anything, and refusal is viewed as deeply offensive. The *hoobae* cannot eat or leave the office before the *seonbae* does. Within the family and among friends, there are also titles of respect, such as *oppa/hyung* (older brother or older male friend) and *unni/nuna* (older sister or older female friend). Coming from this cultural paradigm, my parents weren't about to revise their beliefs to adopt mine; if anyone should comply, it was clearly me. And despite the influence of American culture, a central part of me believed the same thing.

One evening when a friend was leading me through inner healing prayer, I discovered another layer of cultural influence. At one point, we waited quietly to see if God would reveal any generational bondage. Gently, one word materialized in my mind's eye: Confucianism. I had known for a long time that my paternal grandfather had been a deep adherent of Confucianism, but it was only mentioned in the context of my dad's and

1. Dr. Augsburger's term.

his family's eventual conversion to Christianity. It was as if once my father became a Christian, we could assume that any other belief system had been completely supplanted. For this reason, I had never considered how Confucianism might've shaped my father's sense of right and wrong, and thereby mine.

However, during that prayer, it became only too logical that Confucian principles would still hold residual effect. A quick Google search revealed Confucianism's influence on Korean culture and its emphasis on filial piety. It even encouraged the use of shame and comparison as tools to self-regulate and guide moral behavior.

I could definitely see evidence of this in my family and at church. My parents had often used comparison with church friends as motivation, such as telling me how messy my room was compared to my friends' rooms. They'd literally ask, "Aren't you ashamed?" This tendency to gauge success by comparison left little room for alternate pathways. College graduates who landed jobs at well-known, large corporations were a badge of honor for their parents. These young adults were held up as a model to follow. By deviating from this hoped-for course, I *was* ashamed: I felt shame for bringing shame to my parents.

The final layer represents the overarching Korean immigrant narrative that speaks to the many sacrifices the first generation made to provide their children with better opportunities. Leaving their home country and a familiar language and lifestyle, as well as key social networks, my parents' generation had to start from scratch. As a result, many second-generation Korean Americans felt pressure to succeed academically and pursue prestigious, lucrative careers in medicine, law, pharmacy, and engineering to validate their parents' sacrifices. I wouldn't say that our parents believed we owed them, but we felt guilty doing what we wanted when they had given up so much for our sakes.

I remember the following thought running repeatedly through my mind: "My parents have worked so hard their whole lives. Isn't it my turn now to work hard so that they can have a break?" I recognized that the only reason I could even pause my job search was because of the stable financial foundation my parents had created. Yet that same flexibility made me feel guilty. Was I taking advantage of it (as the church members suspected), or was it a legitimate opportunity?

Each concentric layer reinforced my enmeshment with my parents. If that were the end of the story, then perhaps my internal struggle would have been brief. But there is one final layer, not yet mentioned, that encompassed all the others: God.

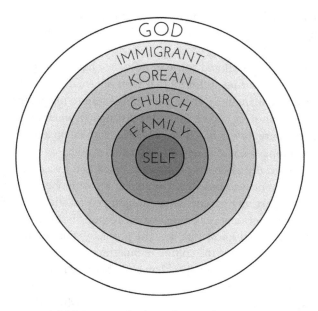

My personal faith journey had taught me that my identity was to come from Christ alone, but the competing layers surrounding me offered conflicting messages. I couldn't help but read Scripture through a certain lens when it came to what I thought it was telling me my relationship with my parents should look like. Not only did "honor your father and mother" make the short list of the Ten Commandments, it was also emphasized throughout Scripture: "Children, obey your parents in the Lord, for this is right . . . 'so that it may be well with you and you may live long on the earth,'"[2] and "If a widow has children or grandchildren, they should first learn their religious duty to their own family and make some repayment to their parents; for this is pleasing in God's sight."[3] A rebellious child could even be stoned to death![4] Though my parents weren't widowed, 1 Tim 5:4 seemed to literally point out my responsibility to pay back my parents' hard work.

Of course, this other verse was usually conveniently ignored: "And, fathers, do not provoke your children to anger."[5] Even though I was aware of it (and similar verses, like "For children ought not to lay up for their parents, but parents for their children"[6]), I couldn't internalize these perspectives

2. Eph 6:1–3.

3. 1 Tim 5:4.

4. Deut 21:18–21.

5. Eph 6:4.

6. 2 Cor 12:14.

to release myself from guilt. The force of the belief systems underlying the competing concentric layers outweighed these underemphasized pieces of information.

Every level of social and spiritual influence had so deeply instilled in me the value of honoring authority that with my small sense of self, it was hard to believe that anything other than submission to my parents was a legitimate, God-honoring choice. I couldn't distinguish whether the disagreement with my parents was based on objective truth or on a desire to justify my own opinions. I couldn't separate spiritual conviction from stubborn selfishness, especially when my parents expressed that I was the latter. Obedience to my parents was practically synonymous with obedience to God.

For their part, my parents were unequipped to release me from my belief that their emotional wellbeing was my responsibility. How could they when they didn't even know that was the problem? Filtered through their lens of Korean culture and the culture of our church, they could not see me as anything other than a defiant problem child because I deviated from convention and failed to conform to their expectations. They could only continue to express their displeasure and disapproval, which then, of course, triggered my basic instinct that I was failing at my very reason for existing.

Identifying the intertwined layers that formed my self-understanding and worldview led me to a breakthrough. The standards I had accepted as normal, universal, and absolute were, in fact, superimposed perspectives of a family, a church, and various subcultures. This warped my understanding of what God *should* be saying in a given situation and prevented me from hearing what God was *actually* saying.

It finally dawned on me why I had allowed my parents' opinions to overshadow mine. With my inconsistencies exposed, the true beliefs that lurked in the murky, hidden plane of my unconscious were brought to light. Learned at such a young age, they were so fundamental that they determined my behavior under duress. The values learned later in life yielded at these critical moments. At bottom, I couldn't truly believe my identity was based only on God's approval because those unconscious, mutually exclusive beliefs had become enshrined as spiritual.

This insight finally broke the cycle of ricocheting between God's voice and my parents' voices. The conflict with my parents was no longer a referendum on who I was at the core of my being. Contextualizing my experience took away the voices that villainized me as a bad daughter or a bad person. It not only brought to light my unconscious beliefs but also disrobed them of legitimacy and any hold over me by giving them a name— much like Jesus stripped demons of power by naming them (and conversely, did not permit them to name him). System, enmeshment, codependency, pseudo-self, culture. These were not God's standards for me, but "demons" that sought to undercut my true source of identity and freedom, which are found in Christ alone.

I had unconsciously made my parents an idol. My parents are godly people whom I respect, but obviously, they are not God. I realized that as a maturing adult with my own faith—and, of course, with the Holy Spirit working in me—I had to make decisions based on my own convictions, even if that meant displeasing my parents. Until then, I had no idea how much the biblical principle of honoring my parents had caused my enmeshment with them to become engraved as spiritual law—so much so that I had sacrificed my selfhood and, ironically, my relationship with God to preserve my relationship with my parents.

God had been right. I had honored my parents more than God, allowing them to define both my identity and God's character. And the most alarming part was that my Christian background had been the very thing that spurred me to do so.

8

A House Differentiated

FORTUNATELY, THE TRANSFERENCE OF emotional stress differs from the conservation of mass in that if it is addressed and resolved, it can dissolve and disappear. Family systems theory also introduced me to the concept of differentiation (or individuation), which helped me to finally break the vicious cycle of enmeshment. Differentiation is the extent to which an individual is able to maintain an identity (desires, needs, thoughts, and emotions) apart from the external influences of social networks, especially family. One's level of differentiation corresponds to one's level of emotional health and capacity for healthy relationships.

This does not mean that complete separation from external input demonstrates optimal emotional health. Often, people pursue freedom from enmeshed families by cutting off all ties and communication, such as by moving away without letting their family know where they are going and refusing to respond to phone calls, texts, or emails. However, this is known as an emotional cutoff and, contrary to appearance, actually reflects enmeshment rather than differentiation (certain abusive or toxic situations are exceptions to this, calling for complete separation).

The tricky thing about enmeshment is that regardless of whether outward behavior reflects independence, the key lies in the driver beneath the surface. If a person's identity is so tied up with their family that the only escape from the pressure of the system is complete disengagement, family expectations can continue to influence motivations and decisions from a distance. If the person were to return, they would immediately be drawn back into the defined family role.

Consider the youngest daughter (let's call her Norma) in a family whose mother married young and became a stay-at-home mom and whose older sisters also married young and stay home with their kids. Norma, on the other hand, has decided to focus on her career, finding technology and computers fascinating. Her family makes her feel unwomanly, flawed, and misguided because she would rather mull over complex mathematical equations than quickly find a husband. She can't wait to get away. She gets into MIT and has never returned home since. As time passes, she's built an established career as the CTO of a Fortune 500 company and has fought for every inch as a woman in a man's world. Everyone in her present context knows her as an intelligent, respected, and confident leader.

Yet when Norma finally decides to reconnect with her family, she finds herself again feeling insecure and small in their presence. She knows rationally that she is smart, competent, and no longer a child to be talked down to—that she is happy with her chosen life. But she feels the need to continually prove this to her mother and sisters amid their conversations about breastfeeding, sleep training, and the latest cutest thing that little Johnny did. Her mother doesn't ask any questions about her work or life, except when she plans on getting married. While circumstances may have changed, the emotional tension remains the same, as she still allows the family's opinions and words to define her. Her need to prove herself reveals her enmeshment because she cannot fully believe her life is good until her family agrees.

Differentiation, on the other hand, empowers a person to remain emotionally engaged with family while maintaining healthy boundaries. They can handle and own their emotions without having to take on the emotions of the family, thus preserving selfhood in the midst of interaction and resisting pressure to return to old patterns of behavior. The individual is allowed to say no, and it is not reactive. Similarly, yes is said out of personal choice, rather than obligation or fear of their family's reaction.

Both conflict and conflict avoidance can be symptoms of enmeshment, but this is not to be confused with the type of conflict resulting from the process of differentiation. As you might imagine, this process can disrupt the family's normal way of functioning. The family may push the individual to return to an established role and subvert—directly or indirectly—their efforts to differentiate. In this scenario, resistance to this pressure is a healthy response. Conflict is not inherently bad; disagreement is not evil.

With Norma, perhaps she starts to grow in differentiation when she realizes her mom questions her life choices due to self-doubt over her own choice of marriage over college—and the resultant lack of confidence in anything outside of housework and child-rearing. Norma then understands that she has internalized her mom's insecurity and she doesn't have to serve as an emotional trash bin. Or perhaps Norma simply realizes that her mom's opinions about the ideal woman don't have to be her own. In either case, Norma is beginning to create emotional separation between her and her mom. As Norma does this, she finds herself better able to handle her mom's comments and her impulse to disconnect from the relationship lessening. She may even draw a further boundary and risk conflict by calmly asking her mom to no longer question her about marriage. This time, remembering she is not her mom's emotional receptacle, she can resist being guilt-tripped back into docility. Or she might choose to answer the question frankly, without anger or even playfully: "Mom, you asked me this yesterday! I haven't had a chance to meet anyone marriable between my bedroom and the kitchen in the last twenty-four hours!"

This lesson of differentiation, once again, gave me a new perspective on the conflict with my parents. I had disrupted my family's equilibrium by not fulfilling my familiar role. Acting contrary to how they were accustomed generated stress and anxiety—the very things I had always tried to alleviate for them. And because obedience was so heavily emphasized in my family, conflict was automatically viewed as wrong. There was no room in the family structure to see me as anything but a rebellious child or for disagreement to be interpreted as an avenue for healthy growth. Seeking my own understanding of what God wanted and how to live my life was simply taboo. However, differentiation reframed all of this, showing me that conflict could actually be a sign of health—the natural process of renegotiating relationships that any family must undergo as children grow to adulthood.

I myself had been afraid I was only being a rebellious child because there was an inner part of me that genuinely wanted to honor my parents, even as I wanted my own identity. I was scared that seeking independence was a full-on adoption of American cultural values over my Korean roots, which signaled rejection of my parents' history and identity—and with that, the many sacrifices they had made for me. It was a lot to be responsible for. The freedom that came from understanding that having my own dreams and philosophy didn't make me a bad daughter exhilarated me. It was earth-shattering! Not only was I *allowed* to disagree with my parents, but it could even reflect health! This didn't, of course, mean I wanted to carelessly fling them aside and live my life irrespective of them. After all, I loved them.

Differentiation showed me it wasn't an either/or proposition. It taught me that having one's own identity wasn't about saying one culture or one way was better than another. It was about having a strong enough sense of self to stay emotionally connected with the system, even if that meant applying some healthy boundaries—to the benefit of all.

When people are healthily differentiated, there is freedom and security to do what they need and want to do. They know what healthy boundaries look like for themselves. They don't depend on others to draw boundaries, and they don't act out of fear of disappointing or being judged. They can make autonomous choices without believing the weight of the system's emotional welfare rests on their compliance.

Inevitably, there will still be times when one will disappoint another in the natural course, but differentiation says it isn't one's responsibility to carry and resolve the other person's disappointment. One certainly should work toward resolution and mutual understanding, but without feeling obligated to make the other happy or spare them from past hurts. There is a vast difference between saying, "I care about you, so I will walk with you, but your emotions are yours and mine are mine," and "I don't want you to feel bad, so I won't tell you what I want," or "You're sad and your sadness is mine." The latter statements internalize the other's emotions, meaning one cannot be happy (or believes oneself to be a bad person) unless the other is also happy. This often leads to a feeling of responsibility to fix it for the other.

At the same time, as the individual relinquishes this savior complex and a dependence on others' emotional condition to feel good about themselves, it allows others to potentially follow the same path of growth. This development in maturity signals to others that they don't need to carry that person's emotions either, and they are given the opportunity to develop their own emotional resilience. This creates an opening for everyone to present their authentic selves and share more honestly. In other words, giving yourself permission to be yourself gives others permission to be themselves. As people cease dancing around each other, guessing at perceived and assumed needs, the collective anxiety level of the system decreases.

I began to see all of this play out in real life. Accepting that obedience to my parents wasn't absolute and that I could disagree with them didn't cause further rupture after all. Rather, it instantly altered the way I related to my parents in a positive way.

For one, it tempered my reactivity to their comments. Instead of hearing everything they said to me as an implied demand or expectation (laced with disappointment at unmet standards), I was able to receive their remarks as suggestions and opinions. I was able to hold what they said in my hands, evaluate it, and come to my own conclusions. I could agree with them without grudging it as I would have in the past out of the sensation that my identity was being subsumed within their desires. Now when I disagreed, a new sense of calm replaced my previous defensive attitude.

As an example, while youth pastoring during my time at Fuller, I asked my dad to help me with a Korean translation for a church activity. As the event approached, I found myself fraught with anxiety, replaying in my mind worst-case scenarios of forgetting what to say or saying the wrong things. As I stopped to reflect on the source of this anxiety, I realized that I had a deep fear of failure (which was, in hindsight, obvious).

After the activity went off without a hitch, I called my dad to thank him for his help and to let him know it went well. I also decided to share about my fear of failure, and the first thing he said to me was, "Why would you be afraid of failing? It's okay to fail." When he said this, annoyance instinctively flared up in me, and heat rose to my face. But this time, I took a step back before reacting, and I could actually track my thought-process shift from one stage to the next in a matter of seconds.

First, I asked myself why I felt annoyed. Second, I realized what I heard behind my dad's words was that I actually *had* failed: "You got it wrong—*again*. You shouldn't have been afraid because you should've known it's okay to fail." Third, I understood that I really just wanted to hear my dad tell me I had done a good job. Fourth, I connected this desire to my need for his approval to feel good about myself. And fifth, I told myself that my identity didn't depend on my dad at all. As I went through this rapid progression, my annoyance dissipated, and I could take the words at face value—it was true, it was okay to fail! I relaxed and simply said, "Yes, Dad."

In the past, my gut reaction would have been to release years of pent-up frustration and say irritably, "I know, Dad! You don't have to tell me that! Can't you just tell me 'good job'?" My dad would've then responded with inevitable defensiveness, reacting (like me) to the emotion in my tone rather than the words, confused as to why I was upset with him when he was just trying to encourage me (in the only way he knew how). Both feeling peeved, we would've changed the subject or hung up to end the confusing tension and never spoken of it ever again. Or I might have simply acquiesced to avoid that very conflict while resenting him inside.

Instead, differentiating myself from my dad prevented a conflict arising from enmeshment. Knowing that who I was did not depend on my dad's response to me resolved my irritation. I understood that the power of defining my identity did not rest in his hands unless I gave it to him. And I didn't have to give it to him—nor did I need his permission not to. With this newfound understanding, I could give up the knee-jerk reaction that was driven by the misplaced feeling that I had never measured up in his eyes.

Differentiation continued to bear fruit in my relationship with my parents. Ironically, being rooted in my own identity made me value and desire to know more about my parents' history. I wanted to see their legacy continue because I no longer carried the weight of resolving their grief from the Korean War, national poverty, and untimely deaths of family members.

I asked more questions and heard incredible stories. Like the time when my grandfather—who, although a farmer, was technically of the noble class—had to be smuggled out of his village by the government because Communists were targeting and killing nobles. Before this, his kind treatment of the labor class had protected him. (It was like watching a Korean drama!) I was struck anew with a deep appreciation and awe, this time without guilt, for all my parents had been through to provide a foundation for me in life. I could finally give free rein to that inner part of me that wanted to honor my parents—who they were and their sacrifices—because I was no longer afraid of losing myself.

New conversations occurred. Instead of getting caught up in the emotional chaos of a disagreement, I had the wherewithal to ask my parents, "What do you mean when you say that?" or "Dad, when you say that we can't communicate because I can't speak Korean, I feel like you're saying I'm not good enough. Is that what you're saying?" Imagine my surprise when he said, "No, I'm upset at myself because my English is so bad." That was clear evidence of how I had absorbed my dad's emotion—had taken an emotion he felt toward himself and redirected it at my own worth.

Learning to differentiate myself from my parents has given me a more balanced approach to life. I want to stay connected to my Korean heritage because I value what it has taught me about the importance of family, being mindful of how my actions affect others, and the strength of character to sacrifice for the greater good. At the same time, I've also learned to shed some narratives drawn from the influence of American culture and Evangelicalism that were limiting my understanding of the "right" life. Catch phrases like "Carpe diem," "Pursue your passion," and "Give 110 percent" blended with Christian rhetoric like "All or nothing for Jesus." Guest speakers urging me as a sensitive and earnest teenager to live as if the world could end at any moment and the ethos of organizations like Youth with a Mission (YWAM) absolutely influenced my approach to the job search. All of this led me to value certain callings and lifestyles over others and to believe there was one best way to follow God. I questioned whether I was truly living for God if I wasn't out in the jungle "saving lost souls" as a missionary or if I didn't continually act out of extreme passion. I wondered if I was too "worldly" and untrusting of God's provision if I had a steady income, saved up for retirement, and didn't donate every dollar beyond absolute necessity to charity. But now with the benefit of a differentiated lens, I can fully respect the quiet faithfulness my parents exhibited in their disciplined execution of everyday, mundane responsibilities.

Under the right approach, it is actually an advantage to be able to draw from both Korean and American cultures, to learn from both and let each inform the other—not in competition but for wisdom. I can appreciate how growing up in the middle of two cultures has, in a way, prepared me to live in the gray areas. It has given me the capacity to connect and empathize with people from different backgrounds.

Ultimately, my job search wasn't a question of who was right. The fundamental problem was that I lacked an identity apart from my parents and was trying to compensate for their emotional wounds, real or imagined. For this reason, I could not say yes or no out of my own agency; I was merely an extension of my parents. However, the simple affirmation that I *wasn't* responsible for their emotions and that I could choose my own path produced a remarkable change in me. I grew in my capacity to genuinely love and honor my parents in heart and action while also honoring myself.

Differentiation propelled me to tremendous personal growth as I began to untangle the mess of my family's expectations, emotions, and mixed messages. Little by little, I was climbing my way out of the invisible maze of enmeshment, which for so many years had bound me in an unyielding trap.

REFLECTION

1. Have you ever experienced tension between what your parents or any other authority in your life wanted and what you believed God wanted? How did you handle it?

2. What cultural influences (concentric circles) exist in your own life and how might they have shaped your understanding of God? How have those influences helped and/or hindered the way you relate to God?

3. Do you see evidence of enmeshment in your own family or church community?

4. What role do you play in your family? How much does this role align with your authentic self and how much of it is a projection of your pseudo-self?

5. How does learning about enmeshment and differentiation change how you see yourself, your relationships, and your faith struggles, if at all?

6. How strong is your own sense of self? How does it feel to say, "I'm allowed to disagree with my parents?" Scary? Obvious? Freeing?

7. Are there any culturally influenced ideas of God that you need to release or reframe?

Part 3

Restoration

"Lord, I'm so stuck. I don't know what I'm supposed to write—where I'm supposed to take this book," I prayed one morning. "You're the one who told me to write this book, and if you don't help me, it's not getting done."

It had already been a year since I had started writing this book, and I had barely made any headway. The task seemed overwhelming and beyond me.

I opened my Bible to Galatians, the place where I was currently at in my daily Bible reading. I read:

> But when Cephas came to Antioch, I opposed him to his face, because he stood self-condemned; for until certain people came from James, he used to eat with the Gentiles. But after they came, he drew back and kept himself separate for fear of the circumcision faction. And the other Jews joined him in this hypocrisy, so that even Barnabas was led astray by their hypocrisy. But when I saw that they were not acting consistently with the truth of the gospel, I said to Cephas before them all, "If you, though a Jew, live like a Gentile and not like a Jew, how can you compel the Gentiles to live like Jews?"[1]
>
> For freedom Christ has set us free. Stand firm, therefore, and do not submit again to a yoke of slavery.

---

1. Gal 2:11–14.

Listen! I, Paul, am telling you that if you let yourselves be circumcised, Christ will be of no benefit to you. Once again I testify to every man who lets himself be circumcised that he is obliged to obey the entire law. You who want to be justified by the law have cut yourselves off from Christ; you have fallen away from grace. For through the Spirit, by faith, we eagerly wait for the hope of righteousness. For in Christ Jesus neither circumcision nor uncircumcision counts for anything; the only thing that counts is faith working through love.

You were running well; who prevented you from obeying the truth? Such persuasion does not come from the one who calls you. A little yeast leavens the whole batch of dough. I am confident about you in the Lord that you will not think otherwise. But whoever it is that is confusing you will pay the penalty. But my friends, why am I still being persecuted if I am still preaching circumcision? In that case the offense of the cross has been removed. I wish those who unsettle you would castrate themselves!

For you were called to freedom, brothers and sisters; only do not use your freedom as an opportunity for self-indulgence, but through love become slaves to one another. For the whole law is summed up in a single commandment, "You shall love your neighbor as yourself." If, however, you bite and devour one another, take care that you are not consumed by one another.[2]

And suddenly it became clear. God spoke into my stuck-ness—I guess God wanted me to write this book after all.

As I read how Peter capitulated to his fear of the circumcision group, I saw my own story. Peter knew the gospel. He was the rock on which Jesus's church was to be built. He had been one of Jesus's closest associates during his time on earth, a member of the innermost part of the inner circle.

He knew that the gospel presented a radically new narrative at that time. It was no longer exclusively through the Judaic law that God accepted a person, which blew the door wide open in terms of who could be "in" and how one got in. It said that somebody—anybody—could access God simply by putting their trust in Jesus Christ, and that trust was enough to make them whole, righteous, and acceptable before God. This meant that Gentiles who believed in Jesus without adopting the whole Jewish law could still be

---

2. Gal 5:1–15.

part of the community of God alongside Jews. Fellowship across cultural lines was now not only possible but the new divine reality.

In fact, God had made this clear to Peter through a vision and a subsequent personal encounter with Gentiles. In Acts 10, Peter received a vision of unclean animals descending from heaven, and God told him to rise and eat. Reluctant to break Judaic law, Peter refused, but the Lord told him not to call unclean what God had made clean. Immediately after this, Peter received an urgent invitation to visit the house of Cornelius, a Greek centurion. He went and encountered a large gathering of Cornelius's relatives and close friends. As Peter shared about Jesus, the Holy Spirit came upon the gathered party, and they began to speak in tongues. When Peter witnessed this, he understood the vision. The Gentiles' receipt of the Holy Spirit showed that forgiveness of sins through Jesus was for Gentiles as well, and it was not up to Peter to dictate who God accepted.

When Peter returned to Jerusalem, the Jewish believers criticized him, saying, "Why did you go to uncircumcised men and eat with them?"[3] But after Peter explained his vision and how the Holy Spirit had descended on the Gentiles, they realized that "God [had] given even to the Gentiles the repentance that leads to life"[4] without requiring circumcision.

Despite this, Peter later wavered when visiting a city called Antioch. When he first arrived, Peter ate freely with Gentile believers, as God had instructed. But once Jewish believers showed up, he immediately slipped back into the old mode in order to appease them. Those people still believed that Gentile believers should adopt Jewish practices, including circumcision, notwithstanding Peter's earlier vision. Peter gave in, quickly separating himself from the Gentiles he had been eating with. What might have caused this turnaround?

In a word: enmeshment.

The new gospel narrative would've required a drastic paradigm shift for traditional Jews. The law represented everything for them: inclusion in family and community, respectability, and national aspirations, as well as spirituality and access to God. Does this sound familiar? These are very similar to the concentric circles I identified within my own faith community.

The law pervaded and defined their lives, especially during their struggle to preserve it during Roman rule—just as my Korean immigrant church community sought to preserve its culture in a foreign country. The Jewish believers followed the rules of the law carefully, thinking this would lead God to restore the prosperity of their nation. So the message that salvation

---

3. Acts 11:3.

4. Acts 11:18.

came through a completely different route (and also looked completely different from the reestablishment of the kingdom of Israel) could not be internalized overnight into a core belief. To uproot their core belief system could very well feel like a betrayal, as if they were treating what once had been precious as trash—tossing God and their people, for whom they genuinely cared, aside. It was certainly a scary proposition. The Jews had depended on their system to live the "right" kind of life. Changing course would have come with the fear that they would cause their cultural unit to fall apart. At a base level—psychologically, emotionally, and spiritually—this would have felt fundamentally wrong.

At first, Peter found it easy to embrace the new narrative because he was surrounded by members of his community who mutually agreed with and lived by it. But once other members who disagreed with him entered the picture, he was pulled back into the old role.

When the challenge comes from within your faith system, by which you have learned to identify yourself and understand right from wrong, the pressure to conform to its rules can be hard to resist. In that crisis moment, Peter allowed self-doubt to drive his decision, forgetting that the gospel had given him the freedom to not be defined by the old ways.

I could indeed see myself in Peter: one moment enjoying the freedom of the gospel, knowing that my identity was not dependent on the expectations or judgments of any social network—then swiftly being pulled back, like a paddle ball yanked by its elastic string, into the doubts of "should" and "should not." I went back and forth, alternating between sweet freedom and crippling bondage.

Paul recounted this story in his letter to the Galatian church, deeply concerned about its confusion regarding the essence of the Christian gospel. He made a passionate case that salvation came through faith in Jesus Christ alone, not from adherence to an encoded system. Paul's firm, public rebuke of Peter's hypocrisy came like a trumpet call that cut through the confusion. With firm finality, it reminded me once again of this truth: it is for freedom that Christ set me free.

I desperately needed to hear this because I was coming to terms with burning out from ministry. As much as the church had taught me about freedom through Christ, it had also deepened my entrapment. Just like the family system, the church doesn't exist in a vacuum. Its message is delivered through human beings who live in a specific historical and cultural context, and the result is a blending of values that come from a variety of sources, not necessarily God.

This had previously confused me, but my newfound insight from Dr. Augsburger's family therapy class enabled me to see shades of gray rather than just black and white. Just because something came from the church or my Christian family didn't automatically make it good or right.

I now had a rubric by which to evaluate the various inputs and to sift through the syncretism in order to distinguish between God and these other influences. Reading Paul's response to Peter crystallized for me the impetus for sharing my story: to declare and celebrate—even through conflict and confusion—that *yes*, God is a God of freedom. It is for freedom that Christ set us free.

9

Enmeshment in the Church

WHILE THE FRAMEWORK OF enmeshment and differentiation gave me a new way to see my family and even produced some significant shifts in my thinking and behavior, I still had a long way to go. I soon discovered how critical differentiation was not only in family matters but also within the church and the world at large. I learned the hard way how dangerous a small sense of self can be in those broader contexts.

When I first moved to LA to attend Fuller, I had no intention or desire to pursue pastoral ministry. In my Seattle home church, nothing had filled me with more joy than investing in the young girls in my small group, so it only seemed to make sense that ministry would be something I'd love to do full-time. Yet whenever anyone asked me if I planned to become a minister, I told them no. I knew I belonged in seminary but sensed God calling me to a non-traditional, yet-unknown path.

Nevertheless, when a classmate approached me one evening and asked if I'd be interested in interning at her church as a pastor, I thought, "Why not? Maybe I should be open instead of automatically rejecting the possibility."

One thing led to another, and instead of my classmate's church, I was connected to her former education pastor at a newly founded Korean church. This church plant already had hundreds of members due to the senior pastor's famed reputation among Koreans. I was hired as an intern for the youth ministry with the presumption that once my internship ended, the youth population would be large enough to support separate junior high and high school ministries. At that point, I would become the designated junior high pastor.

From the first moment I stepped into the church office, apprehension and adrenaline pumped through my body, causing my head to throb. Although there were some overlapping cultural norms with my home church, I could tell right away that the differences were vast. Organizationally, it was like shifting from a warm mom-and-pop shop where everyone knows each other intimately to a sterile megacorporation where you are known only by title and role. Although the church had just formed, it held five separate services for the main congregation, each of which was filled with hundreds of people.

In my home church, I had been taught to focus on relationships and to invest deeply. For instance, during retreats, the leadership team spent each evening discussing and praying over individuals and scheduling personal time for those who needed it. At this new church, such principles ran into the practical limitations of sheer size. While everyone was kind, this world was foreign to me. I desperately sought to exude competency and professionalism like a fish out of water wearing a pantsuit to hide its scales. What had I gotten myself into?

From day one, my tendency to overcommit meant it was too late to turn back, even though the position started out as just a three-month internship. My supervisor's vague future plans for me morphed in my mind into a long-term, binding contract; after all, I didn't want to disappoint him. Events moved rapidly, and I folded myself into the church organization by channeling my over-achieving high school self. The longer I stayed, the deeper I was hooked emotionally—and the harder it was to leave.

I entered my internship like a naïve, doe-eyed girl from a small town who just wanted to make the world a better place. I was wholly unprepared for the unrelenting pull of the continuously turning gears of a large church, and it consumed me.

I would go to bed thinking about my responsibilities and my students. When I woke up, my mind was still racing. On top of a full course load, I met up with several students one-on-one every week. I poured my heart and soul into those students and carried their hurt and troubles with me wherever I went. Their spiritual condition pervaded my thoughts to the point that it spilled out constantly in conversations with my husband and friends. As I learned about their broken home lives, the pressures they faced, and their fears and insecurities, I wanted so desperately to be a consistent presence to show them they mattered—not just to me but also to God. I strove to help them find their anchor, solace, and identity in the security of Christ's love.

Then there were the other seemingly never-ending responsibilities of my position: planning lessons, preparing sermons, tracking attendance, creating bulletins, following up with leaders, and attending prayer meetings and services. Sundays meant waking up bleary-eyed in the dark to attend a prayer meeting with the pastoral staff at 6:00 a.m.; at 7:15 a.m., I sat through the first Korean service at the request of the senior pastor; at 11:00 a.m., I helped with the youth service (and later ran the junior high service); and at 1:00 p.m., I attended the English service for personal worship. Activities that may have been normal for other leaders overwhelmed me; all of the internal space I possessed was already occupied by my anxiety for my students. Whenever I visited Seattle, my parents would look at me with concern, commenting on my wan face.

The burden was crushing me like wheat under a heavy stone mill. My body, mind, and spirit all frayed as though plunged into water, scrubbed aggressively against a washboard, and then cranked through a wringer from morning till night, day after day. My work at this church had sucked the life and joy out of me like a sponge being squeezed tightly to remove every last drop of water—only I was already bone-dry. I wanted to quit.

Over time, I increasingly considered leaving the church. After all, I still wasn't convinced I even wanted to be a pastor! Hadn't I taken the internship to figure that out in the first place? Hadn't I given it a thorough chance? Three months had turned into three long years, and surely this was enough time to develop a well-grounded conclusion.

Despite this, I still couldn't quite pull the plug. I loved my students, and I worried about how they would take yet another pastor leaving. I wanted so much for them to know God as I knew God, and I took upon myself the responsibility to make that happen.

Only in hindsight, long removed from the intensity of the moment, could I see how I had put into practice the enmeshment tendencies of my family and home-church systems in my role as a youth pastor. This led me down a path of inevitable burnout.

Leaving my family and home church in Seattle didn't mean I left the enmeshed system. It was internalized and came with me. It was the lens through which I understood the world and my place in it. Taking responsibility for others' emotions and playing the role I thought the system needed came second nature to me. My shrunken self couldn't hear its own voice or, when it did, instinctively subordinated it to others' voices.

Bringing this lens into a Christian setting can be quite dangerous because Christian values—sacrifice, self-denial, selflessness, and obedience—play right into the hands of enmeshment. Even the language of calling the church a family encourages the projection of our understanding of family onto the church, mutually reinforcing the dysfunction that tends to exist in both systems. As a mentor of mine once noted, Christians can be so much more messed up than non-Christians because of the baggage that comes with growing up in a church.

The problem is not the values themselves. Obedience to parents, sacrificing for others, and many other biblical principles are clearly wonderful things. They offer guidance and a valuable foundation, especially for children, who need concrete boundaries.

The problem occurs when people aren't also encouraged at the same time to develop an identity independent from the system. Growing up in an enmeshed family system plants predefined absolutes, a rooted-to-the-core sense of good and bad, right and wrong. When Christian values do not uproot and transform these definitions through a Christ-centered perspective, but rather build on the faulty foundation of an enmeshed identity, they become yet another set of standards to apply to the pseudo-self for acceptance. The result is that spiritual values are co-opted in order to reinforce the enmeshed system's values, and then a low sense of self stifles any objection. The ensuing vicious cycle keeps our small, unfree selves in an enmeshed trap.

For example, my background had taught me specific enmeshed behavior: avoid confrontation, never say no, refuse help from others, and stay silent about my own desires or needs. I felt compelled to continually "out-give" others, even in situations where my offers to help were repeatedly declined.

Growing up, this behavior seemed to maintain an emotional balance of sorts. If everyone tried to give more than others while refusing help for themselves, then in theory, everyone should be taken care of. This had practical benefits in my family because my parents did, in fact, deeply love me and sacrifice for me, and I reciprocated. My mom especially denied her own needs and labored to provide for me physically and for my education. In turn, I denied my needs and sought to be an obedient, successful daughter who made her happy.

The same pattern played out in my home-church community. I can remember so many situations and conversations that followed this basic outline:

> Person 1: "Can I help you?"
> Person 2: "No, no, I'm fine."
> Person 1: "No, let me help you! I don't mind! I want to help you."
> Person 2: "No, it's really okay!"
> Person 1 then helps without further discussion (perhaps by taking a heavy box out of Person 2's hands, setting up chairs, or doing dishes) as Person 2 protests. Person 1 feels virtuous for going out of their way to help, while Person 2 doesn't have to feel bad for inconveniencing Person 1, since they insisted.

On the surface, these interactions can seem scriptural because we are serving one another. But in reality, they were rooted in a system that required us to take on each other's emotional burdens. There was a heavy imperative to keep others happy and prevent negative emotions like disappointment, embarrassment, regret, or shame. At the same time, relying solely on others for emotional support taught us to expect this from one another. It also deprived us of the opportunity to strengthen our inner selves by learning how to care for our own emotions.

The damaging impact of this dynamic emerged in my new church context, which didn't function in the same way as my home church. As I stepped into my role as a pastor, the new responsibilities and expectations flooded my senses and emotional sensitivity. The fact that I was now being paid for activities I had usually seen as part and parcel of attending church added to the pressure of giving more than I received.

When asked to help with things that weren't part of my position, no wasn't an option in my mind. When I felt utterly exhausted, I disparaged my struggles by comparing myself with others: "Everyone else is doing as much, if not more, than me. Mom worked full-time, cared for four children, *and* served the church every day." Logically speaking, why did my mom's experience have any bearing on whether I was doing enough at my new church? But my enmeshment with her followed me all the way to LA and had become so unconsciously embedded that I didn't even question the soundness of my thought process. I believed I was supposed to work myself to the bone like she did.

I continued to push myself. As I tried to be the perfect pastor, I also tried to fulfill the role of an ideal wife not only for my husband but also his family. I couldn't let myself stop thinking about the troubles and spiritual destinies of my students, but the resulting lack of energy to cook traditional Korean meals (like my mom always had) made me feel like a bad wife. I was torn between guilt for missing any time at church due to visiting my in-laws on special occasions and guilt for cutting our trips short to make it back for church. Many similar things ate away at me, but the crazy thing was that these were not demands my husband actually needed or wanted me to fulfill. They were purely internalized standards absorbed from my concentric circles of enmeshment.

I had no idea how to create boundaries to preserve my selfhood and believed being a good pastor or wife meant deferring to everyone else's needs and wishes—just like I believed deferring to my parents' desires made me a good daughter. I could never really be sure I had done "enough"—to justify my wages, to know my students' struggles didn't result from a break I took, to be viewed by church leaders as a good pastor—because my only metric was everyone else's happiness (and really, how could anyone possibly ensure the happiness of sixty teenagers at any given time?). As a result, I could never disconnect and give myself a break; instead, I continued to give and give and give, unable to ask for or accept help.

Without the built-in scaffolding of my enmeshed system growing up—where someone would carry my emotional burden while I cared for others—I burned out not just emotionally but also physically and mentally. The system that had enabled my small childhood community to survive could not scale to my new church family of hundreds, with people I barely knew. Granted, the church kept us busy; Korean churches are notorious for working their pastors hard. But my low sense of self created a recipe for disaster.

Leaving such an unhealthy context is not as easy as it might seem. My enmeshed paradigm made it impossible to even recognize the unhealthiness of my situation or to validate my desire to leave that unhealthiness. The reason enmeshment is so powerful is because it feeds off a genuine desire to be good. Enmeshment doesn't happen because we don't care; it happens because we *do* care. We care *so* much! To not respond to people's emotions feels cold and uncaring, which is the last thing we want because of how much we care. And God forbid that as Christians we would ever be uncaring when we are supposed to be all about love! Once again, our Christian values play right into the hands of enmeshment.

If the baseline requirement was to out-give others, I viewed any choice for my own welfare as inherently selfish. Even feeling upset became taboo and something to suppress because I was only allowed to think of others. No wonder that even when I wasn't physically present with my students, I was constantly thinking about them and couldn't let myself disconnect mentally or emotionally. I could only be okay if they were okay.

The particularly pernicious aspect of enmeshment is how it self-reinforces by training one to rely on feedback from the system. Our decisions or actions can produce or even just correlate with a negative reaction in our system ("When I came home after hanging out with friends, Mom and Dad seemed exceptionally tired"). From this, we can easily conclude we are not being loving enough ("It's selfish for me to go out and have fun! Mom and Dad need me!").

The church was full of input to keep me in line: a "well-timed" sermon about the importance of spiritual disciplines or sacrifice, a campaign to re-cruit more volunteers, seeing my pastor's fatigue, accountability partners to help us stay "on track." Under such pressure, my genuine efforts to care were always mingled with guilt and anxiety. I could see these triggers then set-ting off cycles that increased the overall anxiety in the group. For instance, accountability can be helpful and has its place, but it can also add to the pressure to perform. When I saw someone "faltering," I would think, "Is it because I didn't call them? Because I wasn't there to listen to their problems? I better check on them now." In response, the other person might anxiously try to get their act together (not out of genuine conviction but in order to appear acceptable) or simply lie to ease my anxiety.

Even if these messages came from innocent, well-intentioned motives, I had already been preconditioned to look to external signals to regulate myself. Unsurprisingly, then, these messages only pushed me harder to perform and perpetuated the pattern of guilt and anxiety.

I wrestled internally for practically the entire three years I worked at this church, but due to my enmeshment, I could not give credence to my reservations about my calling to be a pastor. I looked instead to the system to guide me. And because my spiritual leaders kept telling me I was good at pastoring and didn't doubt that I was called, I concluded I must be a "Jonah," running away in rebellion against God's commands. I chalked up my desire to leave to my own weaknesses.

During that season, "serving God" sucked the life out of me. I accepted exhaustion as a given and thought that being tired meant I was doing something right. I was supposed to suffer, wasn't I? It was only after leaving that I could even consider that maybe this wasn't what Christ meant by denying ourselves and seeking God's kingdom first.

Enmeshment wielded such a strong power over me that it took a clear, repeated directive from God to finally give me the courage to draw the line. I had finally decided to leave the church and had discussed it with the education pastor, but I was still plagued with doubt. When, a couple weeks later, the education pastor urged me to consider staying on longer, I wavered. But as I considered his suggestion, the verses from Matt 11:28–30 leapt out at me from various sources within a span of four days.

The first time, it barely registered. Sitting exhausted in my prayer closet, I read from *My Utmost for His Highest*, the daily devotional book I had used since my college days. That day's reflection contained the reference: "'Come unto Me.' Come, if you are weary and heavy laden. . . ."[1]

Through the fog of my weary mind, I thought to myself, "Oh, yeah, that was the verse I chose for my promise verse this year. I forgot about that . . . I think weary and heavy-laden might apply to me . . ."

Later that day, while randomly scrolling through my Facebook feed, I saw that a former student, in the throes of studying for finals, had posted:

1. Oswald Chambers, *My Utmost for His Highest* (Uhrichsville: Barbour, 1963), 219; Matt 11:28 (KJV).

"Come to me, all of you who are tired and have heavy loads, and I will give you rest."[2] My mind stirred a little: "That's funny, I just read that verse . . ." I typed out a quick note to her: "That's my promise verse for the year. Miss you! *Jahlhae* [good luck]!"

Two days later, on my way to Wednesday night Bible study with the youth, I glanced at the discussion questions for the chapter of the book we were reading. Each chapter ended with a section called "Word Power" that listed verses pertinent to the chapter's topic. One of that day's passages was: "Come to Me, all you who labor and are heavy laden, and I will give you rest. Take My yoke upon you and learn from Me, for I am gentle and lowly in heart, and you will find rest for your souls. For My yoke is easy and My burden is light."[3]

The mists in my mind parted a little as I marveled, "What the . . . ? There it is again. Is God trying to tell me something . . . ?"

The next day, I found myself sitting across from my preaching professor, Chris Tweitmann. I began to share with him my indecision about continuing as the junior high pastor at my church. I told him how I was originally hired to take charge of the junior high ministry, but after my internship ended, they had decided to keep junior high and high school together. So instead, I led a ministry for leadership development that focused on a small group of students. However, once the junior high ministry did split a year later, they slotted in a different intern as the junior high pastor since I was running my leadership ministry. And *then* just a year later, deciding she wasn't a good fit, they had me take over. Now, although I was finally in the position I had originally been hired for, I was ready to be done, but I didn't know if it was the right decision.

After I had rambled for a few minutes, Chris stopped me and said without any ceremony, "Look, I don't think you're supposed to be there anymore. Sometimes, leaders can be selfish and string someone along, even when there's no place for them, because they want to keep good people in reserve for themselves. In my opinion, when the original position you were hired for didn't open up after your internship, that was the time for you to leave. Ministry isn't supposed to be this hard. That's what Jesus is talking about when he says his yoke is easy and his burden is light. It's difficult, yes, but it's a difficulty that feels easy because he gave it to you."

I gasped and held my head in my hands as if to hold it together from bursting as I processed this abrupt culmination of what God was saying

2. Matt 11:28 (NCV).

3. Stormie O Martian, *The Power of a Praying Teen* (Eugene: Harvest House, 2005), 144; Matthew 11:28–30 (NKJV).

through Matt 11:28–30. The fog disappeared in an explosion of light. I couldn't believe what I had just heard.

Hearing Chris tell me so bluntly that I had overextended my stay at this church—through the verses that had been bombarding me all week— hit home a clear message: it's time.

Given the state I was in, nothing less could have released me to finally say goodbye. Because I couldn't yet speak up for myself and pursuing what I wanted and needed still felt inherently wrong, I needed this clear confirmation. God repeatedly smacked me in the face with the verses from Matt 11 until I couldn't miss it.

I had become so deeply buried in my enmeshed identity that I had forgotten that ministry could be life-giving. I defaulted to the conclusion that if it wasn't, then something was wrong with *me*. The notion that I might simply be in the wrong place never even occurred to me. As a result, Chris's suggestion that I could have made my exit after my three-month internship period was never in the realm of possibility. I was still trying to have my cake and eat it too: fulfill the expectations of the system but also pass on the love and freedom I had found in Christ to young people.

What I have learned from this is that being an enmeshed Christian is to be in a form of enslavement—which, ultimately, is an oxymoron. All of the anxiety, fatigue, and second-guessing I had experienced were completely antithetical to the freedom that stands at the foundation of the Christian life. Although faith can be warped into a tool of enmeshment, its true form is the very thing that liberates from enmeshment. Matt 11:28–30 had shown me this.

As hard as it was to tear myself away from my students, I finished my last day at the church. Afterward, I walked back onto Fuller's campus like a woman resurrected. I looked up at the sky and smiled; I had forgotten that the sky was blue. Suddenly, life seemed full of possibility again.

10

Differentiation through Christ

JESUS.

It all begins and ends with Jesus.

Matthew 11:28–30 brought me back to the centrality of Christ—the need to focus my life and identity on him. In doing so, I would receive life even as I gave. How far I had fallen from this fundamental truth despite thinking I was doing Christ's work!

Ministry, once life-giving, had become life-draining. I had thought I was doing what I was supposed to be doing as a loving, faithful Christian. I had always believed that such sacrifice was always vindicated by far greater blessings, like the pleasure and joy of seeing young people grow in intimacy with God. I thought I could merely transpose the way I had done ministry in my home church onto my new church context and see everything unfold in the same way.

However, trying to apply old, enmeshed ways in a new system exposed holes in my prior way of loving. Sacrificial love in the way I understood it worked better in my old church community because it was built into the way we related, everyone unconsciously working to maintain balance in our system. Everyone had gotten the memo: I will sacrifice for others, and they will sacrifice for me. It worked out in that context, but this also meant I never learned to establish boundaries for myself because the system had always done it for me. There had always been someone—a friend, a parent, a sibling—to say, "Hey, you look tired; take a break," or a dinner ready-made when I came home at the end of a long day.

While there were small moments of burnout at my home church, there was enough of a safety net to quickly recover. But in a new, foreign setting, without the collective enmeshed system to fall back on, any spark of burnout was destined to spiral into a free fall.

Clearly, I needed a more robust understanding of what it meant to live and love like Christ—one that stayed true to his purpose to free rather than enslave. Differentiation not only gave me a more nuanced framework with which to relate to my parents, it also blossomed into a new way to care for others in alignment with the way Christ loved. An old lesson, but a new, deeper, and more resonating understanding.

This was one of those moments when my worldview shifted; I felt the Holy Spirit cause information and belief to click into place. Internally, I sensed a deep conviction that this was good and true. It connected theologically and also brought real transformation in my relationships. Family systems wasn't so much about learning psychology, but rather was something that gave me language to express spiritual realities.

The Trinity was no longer some inaccessible, esoteric, doctrinal tenet to be regurgitated by orthodox Christians. Through the lens of differentiation, it tells so much about relating healthily with one another in a practical way. Each member of the Trinity, uniquely separate while also so deeply interrelated that they are in essence one, illustrates the possibility of being united and interdependent without engulfing one another—and independent without isolating or rejecting one another. They have space to move and be who they are but honor each other through integrated thought and purpose—two seemingly mutually exclusive conditions that coexist harmoniously.

In sharp contrast, it had to be one or the other in my family and church systems: either sacrifice yourself to be united or sacrifice community to be your own self. In those contexts, the former almost always trumped the latter. At face value, self-sacrifice appeared to be more consistent with biblical principles, while focusing on oneself automatically seemed selfish. But as I came to learn, the reality is far more complex. Often, the effort to love in this manner was accompanied with resentment and frustration, which paradoxically undermined the desire to love.

In an enmeshed system, what may have begun as a well-balanced mechanism becomes an ensnaring set of unspoken rules and expectations. People talk around each other and walk on egg shells, making accommodations for one another. One can only give so much and rely so long upon others to fulfill needs before the giving becomes obligatory and any perceived imbalance feeds disappointment, misunderstanding, and resentment. A once well-oiled machine can easily spiral out of control as stress and change inevitably enter the system:

I don't really want to do this, but I'll act like I do so she won't be hurt; then surely when I want to do something that she doesn't, she'll do it.

He's telling me he doesn't want to do this even though I want to, and I'd feel guilty if I made him do it; I'll tell him not to worry about it.

Last time, I think she did this for me even though she didn't want to; this time, I should do what she wants to instead.

But . . . I did this for him; why isn't he doing it for me?

I'm disappointed, but I won't tell her so she doesn't feel bad.

Rather than acting out of freely given love, over time strings become attached in this intricate dance that gets more complex and confusing, as well as more restrictive. As emotions build up, the stakes increase. Eventually, boxed into a corner, the two choices appear to be either forcing a complete rupture by lashing out, or staying silent and being swallowed whole.

It is no wonder that enmeshment makes one both resent and protect one's tribe at the same time. It makes people want to simultaneously pull each other closer and push each other away. You want and need each other, and you also desire to be wanted and needed—yet you resent being wanted and needed!

If there is room for only one opinion, a single united identity in a relationship or system, there will invariably be tension over whose will gain supremacy. One cannot "love" without feeling threatened, and one cannot do what's right for oneself without feeling it diminishes the other. This is what happened with my parents. If I persisted in disagreeing with them, I believed I would diminish them by exposing them to the shame of being wrong. But if I gave in to them, while this might fulfill them, I would diminish myself. Only one of us could be right—a destructive zero-sum game.

All I could see was a black-and-white choice between cutting them off to be myself or being engulfed. As I grew and changed—and my parents were correspondingly less capable of providing me with the type of approval and support I needed—the balance teetered out of control. This is literally the stuff that mental disorders are made of. Indeed, the night I forced myself to submit to my parents proved to be psychologically traumatic, leading to a season of depression. How could I be myself without being selfish? How could I love my parents without dooming myself to unhappiness?

This same tension always lurked beneath the surface in my home church. The indirect communication, as well as the accommodations made for presumed emotional needs, came with underlying expectations and unspoken rules for behavior. If not met, disappointment would inevitably follow. And the disappointment could not be vocalized for fear of hurting people's feelings, causing small cracks that would rupture into larger conflicts down the road. By the time conflict bubbled to the surface, the root causes were buried under politics. With the damage so deep and emotions so strong—and no one willing or equipped to speak openly about their feelings—the only available option was a church split. In other words, an emotional cutoff. (When Dr. Augsburger taught us about emotional cutoffs, I gasped inwardly and exclaimed to myself, "There's an actual word for it!") Behavior that had previously bewildered me now made complete sense.

No wonder there was constant comparison within my home church, as we leveraged off each other to bolster our own confidence. Having small, undeveloped selves, we shielded ourselves with external indicators to prove we were good—but always at the cost of another. Without saying it directly, the implication was that I could feel good about myself by comparing my designer brands against your discount ensemble, my house against your smaller one, or my son's impressive salary against your son's modest one. Even my (American-influenced) faith served as a form of leverage and justification against my parents within a relationship where I felt powerless.

While my enmeshment as a youth pastor didn't lead to any outright conflict, it did cause an emotional and physical strain that took a long time to recover from. I basically internalized the damage, and when I left, I implemented emotional cutoffs. Because of my burnout, I was simply not ready to interact with some of the people I had once been so intimate with.

In contrast, as a fully differentiated member of the Trinity, Christ loved sacrificially without ever losing his sense of self. In fact, he obeyed God the Father and loved others out of the strength of his firmly established selfhood. An example of this can be seen when Jesus spends forty days in the wilderness. Satan attacks Jesus's identity by prefacing two temptations with, "If you are the Son of God . . ."[1] Jesus had the power and freedom to choose a different path than that laid out by God the Father, and the temptations were designed to induce him to veer from that path by challenging his identity. Jesus was able to resist because he already knew who he was and had no need to prove anything.

Jesus's act of washing his disciples' feet was similarly premised on the security of his identity: "Jesus knew that the Father had put all things under his power, and that he had come from God and was returning to God."[2] This empowered him to serve in a menial way that shocked his disciples and even evoked protest.

Yet, while he cared deeply and was moved by compassion for the crowds, their emotions never defined him or dictated his actions. Rooted in his identity, he knew what his boundaries were. People praised Jesus and

1. Matt 4:3, 6; Luke 4:3, 9.
2. John 13:3 (NIV).

clamored for his healing and miracles but then turned around and demanded his execution. Jesus displeased the religious leaders, who called him "a
glutton and a drunkard" and disapproved of the sinful company he kept.[3]
Even Peter, one of his closest disciples, rebuked Jesus for saying he would
suffer and die. Peter seemed to understand who Jesus was when he declared
Jesus to be the Christ but became upset when it wasn't on his own terms.[4]
Despite all this, Jesus steadfastly proceeded in his objective. He did nothing in order to earn approval or to protect people from their displeasure.
Neither people's opinions nor the immense pressures of the cultural and
religious systems of his day could deter him from his purpose. But remaining in the security of his identity did not result in alienation from others. In
fact, it was the opposite. He embraced the rejected and marginalized and in
the end, made the ultimate sacrifice out of genuine love.

Jesus did all this—resisted extreme temptations, performed the hum-
blest of tasks, invested in people, and died painfully on a cross—by choice.
His identity as the Son of God did not restrict him; he was not forced to obey
the Father but had true autonomy. He stated explicitly that his life was not
being taken from him, but he was choosing to give his life.[5] His prayer in
the Garden of Gethsemane immediately before his arrest demonstrates this
clearly. He stood before a fork in the road and agonized over the options.
Although he wanted to live in alignment with the Father, he also expressed
his own desire not to go to the cross, interacting with the Father as an independent person. And ultimately, he willingly submitted to the will of the
Father, choosing obedience and the path of suffering out of trust and love.[6]

Viewing Christ's life through the framework of differentiation drastically altered my understanding of what it meant to be and love like him. He
does indeed ask us to surrender ourselves, but he also says that if we lose
our lives to him, we will find them.[7] Could it be that a differentiated self is
what he means?

I believe so.

The reality is that unfortunately, many of us have never been equipped
or encouraged to develop any sense of self. It is a basic human need to be
loved and to belong. But because our parents often lacked emotional security and health due to their own traumas or because their own parents
lacked it, we too begin life with gaping emotional deficits. These types of

---

3. Matt 11:19; Luke 7:34.

4. Matt 16:16, 21–23; Mark 8:29, 31–33.

5. John 10:18.

6. Matt 26:36–39; Mark 14:32–36; Luke 22:39–44.

7. Matt 10:39.

emotional stresses compound over generations when left unresolved. Navigating life in the present is stressful enough on its own, but it becomes exponentially more so when we need to expend lots of energy trying to make up for the past. Seeking to fill these deficits through relationships only further perpetuates the unhealthy cycle of enmeshment into subsequent generations. In essence, we give our lives to others to find ourselves, only to lose ourselves more.

Christ points the way to a radically different relational dynamic in which he does not need us and all our needs for belonging and acceptance are fulfilled. In fact, he loved and died for us before we made a move toward him. In this, I see the convergence of my personal observations from introspection (guided by the Holy Spirit, I trust) with both theology and psychology. At the end of the day, this was the gospel I had learned when I was a teenager, except in a deeper way and with a new frame of reference—its truth told to me from many different angles over time as God met me in ways that corresponded to changing seasons of life.

In our relationship with Christ, there is no obligation, no "I have to," no fear of being either engulfed or rejected. The love of Christ gives us the impetus to stop relying on external validation—those old habits that make us feel loved but also leave us wanting. It provides a foundation for breaking the cycle of enmeshment. We no longer have to carry the emotional burdens of others. Instead, we can entrust them to Christ while also finding the fulfillment of our emotional needs in him.

Through Christ, God invites us to discover our whole, differentiated selves. Christ calls us to die to ourselves, not to become increasingly diminished inside but to receive life. Just as the Father, the Son, and the Holy Spirit are perfectly united and yet maintain three separate identities, we can be affirmed in our identities as God's children without ever losing our distinct sense of self. Thus, counterintuitively, the key to loving others sustainably and sacrificially was to embrace 100 percent, without reservation, my freedom to be myself.

Cue record-scratching sound effect. Wait, what?

Focusing on what I want and think is not only not selfish but helps me love others?

Well, no wonder I had such trouble completely internalizing the gospel.

The promise of the gospel stated that in Christ, I was good, redeemed, and worthy right *now*. That I am and therefore I do, not I am because I do. In other words, I didn't have to act a certain way in order to be good or accepted. I was already good. I was already loving. I was already kind. So I was free to act. Period.

I knew this mentally, but my dependence on a system to tell me whether I was doing okay in life directly counteracted this belief and made the idea of freedom intimidating. The thought of unhindered, unchained freedom awoke intense anxiety in me: "Can I trust myself with freedom? Believing I'm good feels so . . . brazenly prideful. Believing I'm a bad person seems so much humbler. And what if I accept that I'm kind, but in reality, I'm deceiving myself, and I *am* a terrible person? What's going to keep me in check and make sure I'm not running off a cliff?"

There is certainly a risk. Freedom after all is . . . freedom.

Paul agreed that there was ample room within freedom to be selfish. While vehemently advocating for freedom, he acknowledged at the same time that we have every right to choose what to do with that freedom. Because this left open the possibility of inflicting hurt on others, Paul urged his readers to use their freedom to love and serve: "Only do not use your freedom as an opportunity for self-indulgence, but through love become slaves to one another. For the whole law is summed up in a single commandment, 'You shall love your neighbor as yourself.'"[8]

He also warned of the natural consequences of choosing not to love: "If, however, you bite and devour one another, take care that you are not consumed by one another."[9] In other words, we can choose to be self-serving, but we may not like what happens next. In that event, we must take responsibility for the outcomes because they are the result of our choices. On the other hand, Christ living in us means that we will use our power to choose to love and care for others, even when we have equally available the option and right to be selfish.

Could I really trust that Christ not only wanted me to be good (that was easy to believe) but also wanted me to be *free*? Could I trust that I wouldn't take advantage of my freedom to run off the rails and devour others? Could I also trust Christ to be the savior of others so that I didn't have to try to be their savior? This was all too scary to believe until I learned about differentiation.

Differentiation not only showed me that investing in my freedom was, at minimum, not terrible, but also that it could even be *beneficial* for all. If it was just a matter of adopting popular platitudes like "You do you" or "Be yourself," it would not have carried nearly the same weight. Those statements might inspire in the moment, but they couldn't address my deep, primal desire to be safe in relationship—to love and be loved. They couldn't resolve the tension of the zero-sum game that pitted my needs against others'

8. Gal 5:13–14.
9. Gal 5:15.

needs. Differentiation, however, paved a path for me to shift away from my fear of freedom and stride forward in trust. It gave me the courage to begin to remove the braces—that perhaps kept me in check but also formed a prison—because it took into real consideration the impact (particularly the positive one) my independence could have on the community.

For instance, I realized saying no can actually serve everyone. Unconditional love doesn't mean doing things unconditionally for others just because they want those things. In fact, always saying yes might teach them the opposite—that they are loved only when people agree with them, while denial is a rejection of them. And if one says yes out of the fear that saying no makes them an unkind person, the other person can subconsciously pick up on that fear and internalize it. They might come to believe that they, too, must always say yes.

Neither does unconditional love mean protecting people from feeling negative emotions. Seeking to do so by always saying yes can convey that negative emotions, like disappointment or sadness, are so scary and unbearable that they must be avoided at all costs when, in reality, emotions can be managed. In this case, a by-product of avoiding disappointing the other person is a smaller sense of self and weaker emotional resilience in the very person we are attempting to protect—besides the harmful accumulation of resentment in the one who always says yes.

On the other hand, to be able to disagree with someone while still communicating love and a desire to remain in relationship—*that* is a reflection of unconditional love. It provides the opportunity for each person to learn that there is, in fact, a difference between agreement with someone and a person's value.

The tricky thing about enmeshment is that what is communicated implicitly matters more than what is said verbally. Appearances can be deceiving.

As an individual gains the inner resources and maturity to care for themselves, they no longer waste emotional energy on projecting the image they think others want or need—surrendering the burden of protecting others from their own emotions. Being equipped with the strength of one's secure identity and greater emotional margin paradoxically frees one to choose what another person wants out of genuine love.

Suppressed, unspoken emotions are directly addressed or simply dissipate, resulting in greater internal margins for all. As that happens, all are empowered to act out of their free will rather than out of compulsion to care for one another. This results in a community where one can know others and be authentically known. The happy result of healthy differentiation is that more space is created for everyone. Freedom begets more freedom.

I could finally accept the gospel in its entirety—the message of freedom alongside the message of loving and serving others. It was like being liberated from a box whose walls had kept closing in on me ever more tightly until my arms, legs, and neck were contorted around my body in painful, impossible ways. I was released into a sunny, gloriously beautiful meadow full of fresh, reviving air. It made me think of David's words: "[God] brought me out into a broad place; [God] delivered me, because [God] delighted in me."[10] Removing me from a zero-sum mentality, I now had a viable cognitive framework to be authentically myself while also loving genuinely. As I ventured to unfurl my limbs and grew a stronger sense of self, I indeed found that this did not lead to the isolation and rejection of others I had feared. Rather, it made possible deeper and more honest connections.

Choosing to love someone as an autonomous agent is fundamentally distinct from honoring them out of obligation. It was the difference between acting out of my true self and acting out of my pseudo-self. I had already seen the real fruit of this in my relationship with my parents. The economy of God is not a zero-sum game. There is enough space for everyone, just as there is enough space within the Trinity for Father, Son, and Holy Spirit to be both three and one. I too could operate from a place of abundance.

It all begins and ends with Christ. He is more than a mere example of a healthy person or balanced leader. Through his sacrifice on the cross, Jesus opened up to us a pathway to a healthy sense of self. He does ask us to surrender to him and serve others, but not by diminishing or devaluing ourselves. *You have to have a self before you have a self to give,* and Christ invites us to find that self in him and the trinitarian relationship. But even in that, Christ invites, never forces—in full recognition of our distinct selfhood and our freedom to choose.

Christians preach submission and service to others and ultimately to God. But it must always be as a free agent. The source of our love for others has paramount importance. Loving others out of enmeshment keeps us operating from a place of deficit where we are always in the red, no matter how hard we try. It may look like Christian actions on the surface, but it holds us down in the deep seas of fear and anxiety, as if we were trying to tread water with an anchor tied to our ankles.

Jesus says we will know false prophets by their fruits.[11] I already knew all too well that enmeshment generated anxiety, confusion, depression,

10. Ps 18:19.
11. Matt 7:15–16.

shame, anger, resentment, guilt, burden, and burnout in my life. Differentia-tion, on the other hand, harvested the fruits of hope, healing, peace, com-munity, and a greater capacity to extend grace toward myself and others.

Following gospel values out of fear or under compulsion is not the gospel. And this is truly the reason why enmeshment in the church is so dangerous: it proclaims the gospel verbally and projects a message of love and freedom outwardly while undermining it and perpetuating bondage inwardly. In so doing, an enmeshed church undercuts the very message it exists to embody.

I, for one, don't want only the appearance of freedom. I want real, pal-pable, resounding freedom. It is for freedom that Christ set us free.

11

The Process of Freedom

I'LL BE HONEST, THOUGH. Pursuing that real, palpable, resounding freedom has not been easy or as instantaneous as I would like. As revelatory as my time in Dr. Augsburger's class and at Fuller was—and as relieving as quitting my youth pastor position was—it has since been a slow, sometimes painful process of unearthing and reframing false narratives while straining under the push and pull of old and new paradigms. I had no idea then that I was only scratching the surface. The journey of going from a small sense of self to a strong sense of self is hard. Very hard. At least it has been for me.

However, once I began, there was no going back. It was like growing up with a photograph of the ocean, and then, after many years, seeing it in person for the first time. You hear the roar of the water, witness powerful wave crashing upon powerful wave, and gaze out at the vast and compelling openness of the horizon. Salty spray strikes you in the face, and the wind tosses you one way and then another, whipping your hair all around. Having entered the beach with perfectly combed hair and a sense of balance, you will leave disheveled and a little thrown about. But it will also bring a sparkle to your eyes and a spirit that is fully alive, in awe, and simultaneously at peace. A still image could never compare to the real thing. Likewise, I could no longer remain in my enmeshment once I had tasted the freedom of differentiation.

Differentiating myself within my family unit was an easier first step. Not to mention circumstances had changed now that I was married and lived apart from my parents. They had grown; I had grown (and in some ways, I'm sure they felt less responsible for me since I was now "under my husband's care"). But it was quite another challenge to extricate myself from my enmeshment patterns within the church and society at large, and to establish my sense of self in those contexts.

A few months after leaving my youth pastor position, I graduated from Fuller. Suddenly, my life screeched out of warp speed into a snail's crawl. I finally had room to reflect and listen to my soul, consider the causes of my burnout, peel away layers, and allow suppressed emotions and fears to reveal themselves. I started to grope my way out of the dark into recovery.

I went down before going up. At first, the many internalized voices saying what I should and shouldn't do continued to haunt me. I had no job pressures, no degree to be working toward, and wasn't using the degrees I had to any tangible purpose. I had no responsibilities and every opportunity to relax. However, having the luxury to rest distressed me. I wrestled with guilt and feelings of worthlessness. Accustomed to being constantly busy and drawing purpose from high achievement, I couldn't accept my intrinsic worth apart from visible productivity.

My guilt came from the fear that I was indulging myself and therefore being selfish and lazy. All the world around me appeared to be working hard, and here I was, pampering myself with eight to nine hours of sleep a night and sometimes picking up dinner instead of cooking. Never mind that research has consistently warned of the detrimental impacts of sleep deficiency on our health—my social networks had always glorified the physical sacrifice of hard work. I was used to being lauded for giving an excellent presentation or a moving sermon that I stayed up all night to prepare; no one had ever praised me for sleeping eight hours. Even Paul said, "I have labored and toiled and have often gone without sleep."[1] My guilt acted as a self-fulfilling prophecy. It sapped me of energy and motivation to do basic chores around the house and robbed me of quality sleep, making me want to sleep even more.

One day, it dawned on me that the affirmation of others was like a drug addiction. I was taking a walk with a former student when he confessed to me that when he smoked weed, he felt less lonely. His words pierced and exposed my own soul, like in a movie when the camera zooms into a character's eye, showing scenes flashing from one to another as the character finally puts the puzzle pieces together. *Fwoosh, fwoosh, fwoosh . . . light bulb.*

My reliance on my parents' happiness for self-worth had become the model for every other relationship and context. Every word of praise or look of approval, every project and task completed, and every person who depended on me was a "hit"—the feeling you get from a burst of

---

1. 2 Cor 11:27 (NIV).

dopamine—that energized me with a sense of value. But the longer I depended on these things, the more detrimental to my mental and emotional health they became. In fact, it was quite humbling and sobering to realize that the true reason I even entertained the idea of becoming a youth pastor in the first place was my classmate's offhand remark, "I think you would make a good youth pastor." This slight, momentary compliment led me down a path of three years of stress, exhaustion, and depression.

By removing myself from the public eye, I had put myself into a state of withdrawal. Without anyone to please, I couldn't see any use for myself.

This experience revealed yet another reason why breaking out of enmeshment cycles can be so difficult. Separating ourselves from these patterns can be scary because of our dependence on what others in the system provide. We love in order to be loved. We might want space, but the familiarity of being loved in a specific way can make it hard to let go.

It can be tough to be so honest with yourself, but God had placed me in a position that forced me to confront some hard truths. I can see now that even identifying that cycle and deciding I didn't want to live that way was a crucial step toward freedom. I needed to find a new, healthier, more sustainable source of energy and worth.

When my husband and I found a new church to attend, I entered that season prepared to rest and only be minimally involved with the church. Naturally, that meant becoming close with the pastors, volunteering for Vacation Bible School, being appointed to a denominational board, helping lead worship for women's gatherings, and taking on various other informal leadership roles within a matter of months.

In my skewed outlook, because I had no official title, I was convinced that I wasn't doing much at all (particularly because I was still struggling with the fear that I was indulging in too much leisure). But as I gave more and more over time, I found myself yet again overwhelmed by the requests and needs of other people. I still didn't know how to establish boundaries for myself. This time, the fuse was much shorter, and anger at feeling unprotected by the leadership accompanied my fatigue.

We uprooted and began our search for a church once again, and I took more seriously the need to care for myself and become healthy. Something had to change or, at this rate, I wouldn't be able to function in any setting that involved people! In my fear of giving too much and getting burnt out again, relationships became transactional as I calculated how much they had done for me and vice versa. I wanted to hide away from the world forever because I didn't believe I could interact with it without falling into the old patterns and paying enormous emotional costs. Emotional cutoffs had become my default solution. I needed to reassess my role in the church, how to engage there, and how to lead—if at all.

As we visited church after church, I realized I could not step into a church without feeling the pressure to step into my role as a pastor's kid. I heard every announcement asking for volunteers as an indictment that my fear was true: I was selfish and lazy for not helping when others were giving so much. I could not distinguish my parents' voices, my church's voices, societal voices, or all the "shoulds" of being a good Christian from the voice of Christ within me. This led me to decide to take a break from organized church altogether.

In this simple decision (yet radical because of my background), I finally honored my inner self. I was finally listening to myself. I knew clearly that this decision was not rooted in any doubt of the existence of God or a rebellion against faith. I loved Jesus as much as, if not more than, before and wanted to serve him. But the pressure to play the good Christian and the model pastor's daughter continued to drown out all other motives. Others' perceptions (especially those of my parents, who, yes, were deeply concerned) couldn't make me doubt myself. I could see exactly which boundaries I needed to set for myself to step toward genuine freedom, and I didn't have to wait for others to set them for me.

I also began to see a therapist. Knowing that my selfhood mattered to Christ gave me the validation I needed to spend the time and money to get professional help to strengthen that selfhood. Through therapy, I have been able to uncover some of the deep, primal narratives that have defined my outlook. They go even deeper than the need for my parents' happiness and explain why that object has had such a strong hold on my life, even into adulthood.

Two such deep-set narratives emerged. I believed I was somehow fundamentally defective, with my thinking and behavior intrinsically wrong. And I believed my existence made everyone else's life harder. These beliefs were rooted in my trauma as an infant: the death of my biological mother when I was only six months old (a story for another day). No wonder I strove to make my parents happy—my instinct for survival (my "caveman brain," as my therapist calls it) feared being abandoned as unworthy of the space I occupied.

Therapy has helped to literally rewire my brain, accessing the deepest levels of my development and replacing false narratives with the truth and security of the gospel. This process has helped me to stop pretending and to live authentically. The last few years have taught me to know and truly value myself; to see my own voice as valid; to pause and identify whether feelings, desires, and fears are my own or are being internalized from outside sources; and not to automatically dismiss personal desires as evil or less important than other people's wishes.

The healing process required that I risk being selfish—or at least redefine what selfish was. Perhaps even scarier, it required that I risk being *viewed* as selfish. I essentially had to go through the growth cycle of a baby all over again, learning to mother myself by attending to my own basic needs of eating, sleeping, and emotional safety. This meant saying no a lot more because a baby isn't expected to care for others but instead is cared for. In doing so, I discovered the richness of my own inner resources and strength to tell me who I was, rather than depending on the external validation of others.

Over time, with a developing voice and sense of self, my boundaries became less porous. I realized I didn't need to be everyone's best friend or a revolving door for everyone's opinions and emotions. Instead of absorbing others' feelings or taking their reactions as a statement on my identity, I could identify what was theirs and give it back to them.

For example, I now approach social situations differently. In the past, I was scared of coming off as rude or incompetent when meeting new people. This led me to always measure my words carefully and self-consciously (while second-guessing everything I said or did), or to just exclude myself from the conversation altogether. Unsurprisingly, this made me dread gatherings with strangers.

Understanding that I don't need others' validation—that I can validate myself and start from the premise of my intrinsic goodness—has changed this pattern. I began to enter these social settings with the confident thought, "I'm not a rude person—I'm a kind person." Even if I happened to do something that was accidentally rude or could be perceived as rude, I could rest assured that others' judgment didn't actually make me a bad person (as if—*poof!*—a wizard might instantaneously transform me from a human into a hideous monster with a wave of his wand). Meeting new people and entering unfamiliar situations became more relaxing and easier to navigate as I realized, "Their opinion is theirs, and it doesn't have to matter to me."

This was a huge step forward. Previously, I had always started with the premise that I was bad. In a form of self-flagellation, I would deprecate myself in order to force myself into submission—to make myself more amenable to sacrificing myself for anyone and everyone (thinking, for example, "The reason you feel annoyed is because you're mean and inconsiderate; you should just accommodate her because that's the nice thing to do"). In this way, loving and serving others also meant tearing myself down. It was always an impossibly lopsided balancing act, which left me increasingly depleted and literally fearful of human interaction and commitment.

Believing in my own worth and letting myself begin at one hundred—rather than negative five hundred—tapped into fresh and renewable resources for relationships. I didn't need other people's validation—I could validate myself! It was no longer "I will do this for her because what I desire isn't as important as what she wants" or "I don't want to do this, but not only should I do it, I should *want* to" (implying something was inherently wrong with me for not wanting to). Instead, I could say without resentment: "Although I want something different and that desire is equally valid, I will do this for her because I choose to serve her this way."

As I've learned to depend less on others to validate me, strengthening my own voice has made me a safer person and better listener for others. Others don't need to artificially adjust to my need for them to be a certain way in order for me to feel good about myself. The more comfortable I am in my own skin, the more comfortable others can be in theirs around me. I'm no longer trying to protect and prove myself or impose the enmeshed system's values. Now I can give space for others to discover their own voice and for God to work in their lives.

Thinking back on my past voice, especially in chapter 5, makes me cringe because I can hear the judgmental and arrogant tone emanating from those words. My growth has opened my eyes to the beauty and admirableness of my parents' generation's way of practicing their faith. Having released the grip of emotional responsibility and being free to say that it doesn't have to be my way, I can see that God is in their worship, just as God is in mine.

For instance, I'm pretty sure I'll never love or commit to early morning prayer service the way the Korean church does. Frankly, I can't function well the rest of the day after waking up as early as 4:30 a.m. In the past, my avid dislike for these predawn services made me feel undisciplined and lazy—I wondered why I couldn't be as enthusiastic as others. At the same time, I also criticized it as a legalistic practice because people seemed to equate one's commitment to it to the maturity of one's faith. However, I suspect a lot of my prior criticism came out of a need to make myself feel better about myself. I can now readily respect the practice because I realize that not attending early morning prayer service doesn't make me a bad Christian or a bad person. In fact, I am grateful to know I have access to a whole army that will powerfully and corporately pray for me if I need it.

Strengthening the emotional boundaries around myself didn't mean shutting out others or never listening to others' opinions. While I no longer had to wait for others to fulfill my needs—and I stopped holding them to that expectation—this wasn't about saying, "I don't need anyone's help!" or "What anyone else thinks doesn't matter at all!" On the contrary, developing my own voice has helped me discern which voices to let in. I've come to realize that the voices I should trust the most are the ones that would never undermine my autonomy, even if they also challenge or disagree with me, and will always remind me of Christ's love when I need it. God's voice through Scripture and the Holy Spirit will always be primary here, and my spiritual disciplines have been all the more precious and indispensable during this season. Pressing into Christ's presence—simply sitting in quiet before him daily and listening—keeps me centered and grounded in truth about who I am, what my purpose is, and where I should give.

It's also helped me be more honest when I need help or feel hurt. Because I'm not secretly hoping someone will rescue me and I'm not trying to manage someone else's emotions, there is less at stake—less pressure both for me and for whoever I ask for help. As a result, it's given my husband, family, and friends the opportunity to love me in the ways I actually need, and vice versa. These relationships have grown in honesty and trust as I have encountered love and acceptance that endure despite the exposure of my deepest vulnerabilities—and reconciliation when there is conflict.

As I have learned to cast off the lies of enmeshment and strengthen my inner self, I am finding the courage and desire to engage with the world returning again (admittedly, very slowly!)—but not at everyone's beck and call. I now understand that time alone with my personal interests and needs is okay too. I find myself surrounded by a husband, family, and friends who really know and support me, and whom I can also support in turn. I am ready to be faithful where God has called me to be and to trust that is enough, no matter how small or mundane.

I am nowhere near out of the woods. There are days when I talk to God and say, "But shouldn't I be out there *doing* something?" and God continues to tell me to wait. But ultimately, I am grateful to have had this season of quiet and healing.

It's a day-to-day process, but that is something else I have learned from all this: the confidence that comes from fully internalizing the gospel enables me to accept the reality that I am not perfect but rather in process. This is, in and of itself, a freeing concept. I had known that the journey mattered to God and that God wouldn't judge me over a single moment. But this was yet another aspect of God I had believed only superficially, something demonstrated none more starkly than at the conclusion of my job search. At that time, I quickly reverted to an outcome-based theology that reduced God to a black-and-white, vengeful God who blessed when pleased with me and punished when offended.

I think many of us have ideas of what life is supposed to look like. These narratives spring from society, culture, upbringing, religion, and more—and we look to such external cues to let us know we have arrived.

Even after learning about family systems, I could've used that information to look back on the conflict with my parents and say, "I shouldn't have given in to their pressure"—letting it become another cause for shame, a new narrative that presented another standard that I failed. Instead, I look at it as part of my overall trajectory. I didn't know then what I know now. Maybe it would've been nice if it hadn't happened at all, but it did happen—and so became a building block toward who I am now and who I will become.

When I was a teenager, I used to think that when I struggled with faith, this meant that God was far away because I had little faith. And conversely, when I passionately expressed my love for God, I thought God was near because I had a lot of faith. Now I can see God was always near. God is always present because God *is*. My emotions can't change God; it was more that I had to grow to fit the reality of what already was.

Even this book represents that. I am not the same person today writing this section as I was when I wrote chapter 5. Time and again, from the first day God called me to write this book, I struggled and doubted, allowing myself to be distracted by other projects with more tangible results. At this moment, I have no idea whether it will ever be published, who will read it, and how people will react to it. I struggle with validation that lacks external markers like salary and the vindication of publishing. But I am here—pressing forward in faith and trusting in the process—to complete this book, whatever may come.

There's something incredibly freeing, grace-filled, and *spacious* about looking at the world through the lens of process. It helps me practice self-compassion and release others from unfair demands. I am able to recognize that as complex and multilayered human beings, we might be in different places, and it might take time to find where we intersect. Even relationships are in process; conflict represents just a snapshot in the larger arc, not definitive of the whole—just as the conflict with my parents when I was twenty-two didn't mean we were doomed for all time (although it felt like that at the time!). As I put my trust in God's faithful, unchanging character—that God is the one who works and transforms—I realize I'm simply along for the ride.

My constant prayer now is one of surrender, that Christ might increase and that I might decrease. It's interesting how growing my sense of self has actually magnified the desire for more of Christ and *less* of me![2] I know that ultimately, it is only in Christ that I find my true self and fulfillment.

Jesus's words from John 15 have continually come back to me throughout these past few years: that true fruitfulness and productivity come from simply being in relationship with Christ.

2. John 3:30.

I am the true vine, and my Father is the vinegrower. He removes
every branch in me that bears no fruit. Every branch that bears
fruit he prunes to make it bear more fruit. You have already been
cleansed by the word that I have spoken to you. Abide in me as I
abide in you. Just as the branch cannot bear fruit by itself unless
it abides in the vine, neither can you unless you abide in me. I
am the vine, you are the branches. Those who abide in me and
I in them bear much fruit, because apart from me you can do
nothing.[3]

I pray to take responsibility only for those needs that God calls me to
help with and to be discerning and wise. It is difficult to turn down opportunities. Needs are everywhere, and unfortunately, there will always be people
who will judge you when you decline to help with those needs. Our modern
era of hyper-connectivity only amplifies this pressure. However, I know that
chasing every need has only succeeded in making me spread myself too
thin, leading me to crash and burn in every role I've taken upon myself. And
rather than forcing change or insisting on an established system, I want to
speak and act within the rhythms of God's movements.

God is not finished with me yet, but I trust "that the one who began a
good work [in me] will bring it to completion by the day of Jesus Christ."[4]

3. John 15:1–5.
4. Phil 1:6.

REFLECTION

1. Why are you doing what you are doing? More than what we do or what we say, *why* we do it speaks volumes.

   - Does it make you feel guilty if you don't do it?
   - Does it make you fearful if you don't do it?
   - Does it make you anxious if you don't do it?
   - Does it make you feel like you're in a deficit if you don't do it?
   - Reminder: these are not fruits of the gospel.

2. To what extent do you rely on feedback from others for your identity? To tell you that you're doing okay in life?

3. What cultural and subcultural influences exist in your life that indicate to you what and who you are supposed to be? Whether you are good or bad? To what extent do these influences align or not align with the gospel of freedom? Why or why not?

4. On a scale of 1 to 10, how porous are your boundaries? Do you think you could say no more often? Do you think you could say yes more?

5. Does it feel selfish to "be yourself" or to apply boundaries around yourself? How might the idea of differentiation and the life of Christ help you reframe this?

6. Has faith been a source of freedom or oppression for you? If oppression, how might working toward a stronger sense of self change this? How loud are external voices compared to your own inner voice and the voice of the Holy Spirit within you?

7. How can you create space in your life to listen to Christ's voice (if you haven't already)?

8. Who are the voices in your life that you know you can trust, people who really know you and will not force you to diminish yourself even as they give you honest feedback?

Epilogue

BOTH PETER AND I could have told anyone what the gospel was if they had asked us, and I'm sure we both shared a genuine desire to faithfully follow God. Thus, it was initially disconcerting and confusing to realize that despite experiencing the freedom of the gospel, my very desire to be faithful to God unwittingly drove me to behavior that *wasn't* faithful to God—and trapped me in patterns of guilt, shame, anxiety, and fear, rather than freedom from those things. This ultimately led me to question the very character of God.

I believe God wants me to share my story in order to demonstrate how enmeshment can mimic Christian life while undermining its core message of freedom. My hope in writing this book is that it will serve as a reminder that it is for freedom that Christ has set us free and that it will help people experience that freedom more profoundly.

I think many people may be struggling internally without realizing the greater forces at work, seeing only symptoms rather than the root causes. They might be asking why the same negative cycles keep recurring when they know better, and when they know God loves them. They may be asking why, despite their best efforts, they find themselves once again burnt out, depressed, or indulging in bad habits.

I would like to suggest that perhaps there is a different way of understanding those difficulties. The cause might very well be enmeshment in their systems, and if so, the framework of differentiation can help.

In Galatians, Paul reaches back to Abraham to demonstrate that faith has always been at the root and vision of God's work in God's people. The law was a temporary measure until God's plan reached its fulfilment through Jesus. Faith is meant to move us from within. The law, in stark contrast, was an externally imposed system that could dictate behavior but could not change hearts. This was why every new generation of Israelites fell away from God in pursuit of other gods.

While following a set of rules may modify behavior to a certain extent, it can also create a system of bondage. Do you have to follow every single letter of the law to be okay? Are you doing enough? Does a mistake in one area undermine everything else you did right? These questions leave people in a state of insecurity, leading to a need to achieve and perform to obtain security. This system also reduces the relationship with God to a transactional and moralistic one: God will bless me if I obey and punish me if I don't. It is a relationship based on fear, while faith is a relationship based on trust.

This dynamic of the law is evident beyond the belief system of Old Testament times. Our social systems are built in such a way that they constantly dictate what you must do to fit in and be accepted. The consequence of ignoring those rules is rejection. The pervasiveness of social media only intensifies this.

In such a setting, freedom is all the more difficult to internalize if it is also undermined by the spiritual weight of church systems. The church, with its origin and institutional purpose arising from the gospel, should be on the front line teaching that our identity comes from Christ alone. But this message of freedom can stealthily shift into a message of bondage. We don't even recognize it is happening because the same types of standards are used in all other parts of life. The law feeds directly into human nature. We want clear boundaries so that we know the minimum we need to do to be okay—it's efficient. We also like feedback and the approval of others—it feels good.

Efforts to avoid legalism or to establish an ideal church often result in the creation of systems that themselves become legalistic. For example, the evangelical church has roots in the Protestant Reformation, a movement that began when Martin Luther excoriated the Catholic Church for its legalism. Since then, Evangelicalism has emphasized that one is saved by faith, not by deeds. But legalism can just as easily exist within evangelical settings, such as when, for instance, there is tacit pressure and judgment surrounding the amount of time a person should volunteer. Conversely, a Catholic church, with its highly structured traditions, can be free of legalism when members are serving joyfully and autonomously. As I once heard, our practices should point us to God, but God is not our practices. The form matters less than the unspoken expectations underlying those forms.

Legalism functions a lot like enmeshment, and once we understand that, we can detect why we might be struggling with certain unhealthy patterns. Better yet, we know the antidote: differentiation. It's not about depending on the system (or law) as one's rubric or creating a perfect system devoid of legalism; it's about not needing a system at all. Or perhaps more to the point, being able to function in *any* system (since to be human is to inevitably be a part of systems) as a healthy, differentiated self.

As Paul called out Peter, I want to make a special note to leaders—almost a plea—to be much more aware of and cautious with the influence they wield. I believe healthy organizations have healthy leaders who grow a healthy sense of self and encourage their followers to do the same.

It might seem like Paul overreacted by calling out Peter so publicly, but he recognized that threats to the gospel did not need to be drastic: "A little yeast leavens the whole batch of dough."[1] Paul perceived it was more than just an issue of whether Jews and non-Jews could eat together. It was that the very essence of the gospel was being jeopardized—from the highest and innermost level of authority—by an original disciple of Christ, no less.

For this reason, Paul's strenuous warning to the Galatian church and encouragement to stand firm appears absolutely warranted. Unfortunately, there's more than just a little leaven attacking the freedom of the gospel in our families and society today, and too often it comes from within. When opposition comes from outside the faith community, it's a difficulty one takes for granted. For example, Christians are taught that it's *supposed* to be hard in school, in work, and among non-Christian friends—people are *supposed* to disagree with you there. Sometimes, that kind of opposition actually entrenches you more deeply in your distinct identity, just as Roman rule made the Jews more entrenched in theirs. However, if the leaven comes from within, it can be hard to identify it for what it is. Understanding differentiation can help us be vigilant in continually re-centering ourselves in the truth that it is for freedom Christ set us free.

Looking back on my own experience, my home church did equip me with many of the teachings and tools that enabled me to eventually understand the enmeshed church dynamics that stood in the way of true freedom. Ultimately, however, on this side of heaven, the church will always be subject to the influence and input of cultures and subcultures in the environment within which it exists. It is composed of people who bring with them their own norms for behavior, as well as those of generations past. As a result, the church absorbs elements from each of these norms and, over time, takes on a collective identity with both spoken and unspoken values, beliefs, and expectations.

Consequently, the institution that is meant to draw us near to God can actually make finding God harder—for the very reason that it is trying so hard. A genuine earnestness to love God can result in rules designed with the well-intended purpose of achieving that goal. But invariably, the demand for strict adherence to those rules will end up obscuring the ultimate aim of loving God—missing the forest for the trees. In this way, the church

---

1. Gal 5:9

has often tragically been the perpetrator of oppression rather than an agent of liberation and healing.

I still value the church and believe in it as Christ's body (yes, I am attending church again, and it feels completely different!). But I suspect the church would benefit from some deep reflection on how enmeshment may be playing a mischievous part in limiting people's spiritual growth. We can all be vulnerable to enmeshment, with numerous and varied root causes. The underlying narratives that drive us often lie in our unconscious, and we unknowingly project those stories onto others.

For leaders, it is especially important to understand their driving narratives and those operating in their organization. Just as emotional stress can be passed through generations, it is also transmitted from leaders to an organization's members. If we are anxious leaders, those in our care might feel compelled to take care of us, and so rather than growing spiritually, they may merely be seeking to fulfill our emotional needs. It is a great responsibility to be in any position of influence, whether as a parent or leader. Being healthy emotionally is crucial both for one's own sake and also for those over whom one has influence.

When I left my youth pastor position, I initially worried about my students feeling abandoned or believing that I didn't care about them. Looking back now, I think the bigger issue was the example I left behind. For instance, I could encourage the young volunteer leaders who helped me with the junior high ministry to rest, and I could check in on them to make sure they weren't taking on too much. But *only while I was there.* And no matter what I told them, if I didn't rest and never said no myself, I indirectly undermined my own message. I didn't model to them how to take care of themselves. I only perpetuated the pattern and, by my example, set them up for burnout. Like Peter, leaders who are susceptible to enmeshment will bring their followers into the fallout with them. What we model is more important than what we say.

Don't get me wrong, though. What we say matters too. I recently heard someone preach on sin and how we need to be skeptical of our desires. When I was younger, I would have lapped up such a sermon. But having gone through many changes the past few years, it didn't sit well with me. Now understanding the powerful influence of enmeshment, it occurred to me that encouraging listeners to be skeptical of themselves may be reinforcing their small sense of selves. This could leave them vulnerable to their leaders' (or others') authority becoming absolute, reinforcing their reliance on others to tell them what to do and whether they are good or not. The enmeshment cycle and all the issues it entails would thus grow stronger. Is that what we want as leaders?

It's not that I think all our desires are praiseworthy or do not need guidance. But I can't help but wonder if we are missing the point, still more preoccupied with making sure people don't do something wrong than restoring their Christ-given identities. Is it possible to get to a place where I no longer need to be skeptical of my desires? Perhaps instead, my desire for Christ can grow and mature to eventually supersede other desires, and my natural choices will fall in line with God's will. What would it look like to empower others toward this end, rather than filling them with even more self-doubt? What if we could guide them to trust deeply in their relationship with Christ and the indwelling Spirit to keep them in line with God? Isn't that the transformative freedom of the gospel?

As leaders, we have more power than we know. As a person with a small sense of self, this was unimaginable for me, and I learned the hard way how influential my approval could be. When we are in a position of authority, what we may simply see as suggestions can be received as law by our listeners. Just recently, speaking with a mentee, I realized I needed to stop giving her advice and instead encourage her to seek God's voice for herself. That temptation to offer solutions—to ease her pain and my anxiety—was preventing the strengthening of her own voice and connection with God. While I had always advised her to trust that the Spirit lived in her and that God would speak to her, my impulse to give her answers communicated the opposite—that she should listen to others (like me) instead of the Spirit's voice within her.

Even though I had told her she was allowed to make mistakes because God's grace was enough, my tendency to give solutions communicated that she actually wasn't. Without the actual space to try and be wrong, how could she learn to distinguish Christ's voice? Learning to have a stronger sense of self gave me the ability to resist jumping to her rescue, but it took great self-restraint! I had to be aware of and resist the temptation to feel useful, helpful, or productive. I had to accept that she may not get it right the first time or that there might be no single right answer.

Admittedly, freedom is a lot messier and riskier than maintaining the system. Teaching people to follow rules is a lot easier than walking with them and teaching the why behind values, hoping they come to own their faith. It takes a lot more wisdom, patience, discernment, nuance, heartache, and time; it is much easier to apply a one-size-fits-all approach.

But I am convinced we must offer the space for people to figure things out, make their own choices, and not be artificially protected from the consequences of their decisions. This certainly comes with the risk that, despite a leader's sincere efforts, people may decide to walk away—or worse, make choices that lead to self-destruction. In those situations, only a deeply rooted identity in Christ can reassure one not to equate the spiritual condition of followers, or the church as a whole, as a reflection of one's worth. We can do so much simply by ensuring that we ourselves are healthy people and by increasing our self-awareness.

REFLECTION FOR COMMUNITY

1. How might we be placing the yoke of slavery on each other through our expectations and preconceived ideas of what following God should look like or what our lives should look like?

2. What unspoken rules exist in our system? Are those consistent with the gospel of freedom? Why or why not?

3. How can we be a living reminder to one another that it is for freedom that Christ set us free?

REFLECTION FOR LEADERS

1. To what extent are you truly freeing those you lead to be who God created them to be? Or are you merely teaching them to follow rules and reinforcing their need to project pseudo-selves?

2. How much do you need the approval of others to make you feel like a good leader?

3. Are you inserting people into an existing system—a system that is really just your own best effort at an interpretation of what church is supposed to look like—or teaching them to discover their own place in the kingdom of God?

4. Are your ideas about God and church more important to you than encouraging your followers to press into knowing and encountering God in real ways? Do our practices serve us or do we serve our practices?

5. Are you willing to suspend judgment and be wrong about what you think you know?

6. How do you feel about your value when you are not leading other people and not in the spotlight?

7. How much does your inner life align with what you say to those you lead?

8. How might enmeshment within your church/community be restricting people's experience of freedom in Christ?

9. How can you encourage others toward strengthening their sense of self? How might you be undermining their development in this area? Are you modeling healthy boundaries to your followers?

Appendix: Resources and Next Steps

PERHAPS YOU ARE AWAKENING to the realization that you are enmeshed with your family and your church, and you are asking, "What next?"

In reading my story, I hope you have been able to extrapolate and synthesize some ideas of what might facilitate your own journey of healing and freedom. I truly believe that *awareness* and *acknowledgement* in themselves go a long way.

I would also like to offer some practical tools to help you become more in tune with God's voice regarding your identity in Christ. They are not particularly novel or earth-shattering; the goal is to ultimately utilize whatever tools will help you internalize to the innermost depths of your being the truth of who you are as God's child—forgiven, redeemed, and freed by Christ. This is why some knowledge of psychological tools and how the brain functions can help.

Please remember that healing is a *process*. It takes time. I've often felt like I took two steps forward only to then take one step back, but over time, the small shifts accumulate to form a renewed you.

IDENTIFY AND REFRAME FALSE NARRATIVES

I have become an unapologetic self-talker. I talk to myself and do so liberally. The fact is that you're probably already talking to yourself in your mind about who you are and how you should act, but it's so subconscious that you don't even realize it's happening. Thoughts flash through our minds so automatically—tracing the familiar grooves in our brains and becoming a part of our psyches—that these thoughts don't register as thoughts, but as fundamental, logical, and universal truths. I call these narratives—stories we tell ourselves about who we are and how we should interact with the world. They take root and germinate when we are children—infants even—so that by the time we are more fully conscious of ourselves, they are already a part of us.

Unfortunately, some of these narratives are unhelpful for living a life of freedom and grace, but because they are so core to us and feel like Truth with a capital *T*, it can be hard to separate ourselves from these beliefs. It is not simply a matter of saying we believe something else; the false belief has to be uprooted.

To do this, I had to learn to listen to my own thoughts and what I was saying to myself, especially in scenarios that provoked my anxiety. When I made a mistake or even simply walked into a room filled with unfamiliar people, I detected thoughts like "Argh, I am so bad at this!" and "What people think about me defines my goodness; therefore, what they think matters, and I need to ensure they like me." As I got better at hearing my own thoughts, I could then treat them more objectively and consider whether they were false or true, and whether they conflicted or aligned with what I said I believed.

Below, I demonstrate the process I followed to reframe self-sabotaging beliefs. First, I identify a false, restrictive narrative that I had absorbed. I then show contextual inputs that shaped that underlying belief, as well as the biblical references that reinforced and spiritualized those beliefs. Then I show why the narrative is false within a gospel paradigm. Finally, I select a phrase or short prayer that I meditate on to help center myself in the new, gospel-based narrative. This is especially helpful if I find myself triggered and defaulting back into the old pattern. To help deconstruct some of your own false narratives, feel free to follow the same process.

False Narrative:

The only way I know I'm doing enough is if I'm exhausted. Otherwise, I'm lazy.

Contextual Input:

One of my parents' favorite things to tell me was "*Bujeoreonheehae*," which meant, "Do it diligently and efficiently." A leisurely lifestyle was simply not something to emulate or aspire to. My parents scolded me for sleeping in during summer vacation, but when they saw me pulling all-nighters for homework, they became soft, kind, and concerned, telling me to sleep as soon as I could. I often felt guilty if I was out having a good time with my friends while my parents were stressed out and tired at home. Furthermore, it just seemed like all the adults at church were perpetually exhausted, bearing heavy burdens and working hard in the small businesses they owned—in addition to their diligent involvement at church.

Spiritual Input:

Paul seemed to exhaust himself to do God's work:

> "Are they ministers of Christ? I am talking like a madman—I am a better one: with far greater labors, far more imprisonments, with countless floggings, and often near death. Five times I have received from the Jews the forty lashes minus one. Three times I was beaten with rods. Once I received a stoning. Three times I was shipwrecked; for a night and a day I was adrift at sea; on frequent journeys, in danger from rivers, danger from bandits, danger from my own people, danger from Gentiles, danger in the city, danger in the wilderness, danger at sea, danger from false brothers and sisters; in toil and hardship, through many a sleepless night, hungry and thirsty, often without food, cold and naked. And besides other things, I am under daily pressure because of my anxiety for all the churches."[1]

Why This Is Inconsistent with the Gospel:

Scripture is replete with the imagery of God as our rest and refreshment. Psalm 23 speaks of how God leads us beside still waters, refreshes our soul, and causes our cup to overflow. In addition, Jesus declared that he came to give life abundantly[2] and described life as a gushing spring[3] and a flowing river.[4] It brings to mind an eternal oasis. Exhaustion, on the other hand, evokes the opposite imagery: drought and scarcity.

Furthermore, Paul's "boast" must be read in its context. He wasn't actually boasting. He was confronting the Corinthian church (who didn't find him as captivating or powerful as certain "super-apostles") for questioning his legitimacy as an apostle of Christ.[5] In the end, he said that only his weaknesses were worth boasting about, not how much he did or the spectacular

---

1. 2 Cor 11:23–28.
2. John 10:10.
3. John 4:14.
4. John 7:38.
5. 2 Cor 11:5.

spiritual experiences God gave him, because they further emphasized the grace and power of God.[6]

Ultimately, Christ calls me to move from a place of grace rather than fear. The way to know I'm doing enough is to know that Christ's grace is enough. It's about his work, not mine.

Phrase or Verse to Counter This Narrative:

"You lead me beside still waters; you restore my soul."[7]
"It's about Christ's work, not mine."

To help deconstruct some of your own false narratives, feel free to follow the same process:

False Narrative:
Cultural Inputs:
Spiritual Inputs:
Why This Is Inconsistent with the Gospel:
Phrase or Verse to Counter This Narrative:

6. 2 Cor 12:9.
7. Ps 23:2–3.

THERAPY

Some cultures view therapy with suspicion (as unnecessary or a breach of family loyalty), preferring to keep private matters within the family. At the most, they might permit consulting with pastors and spiritual leaders. Sometimes, it is a leap to accept that one might need the help of a therapist because one thinks he or she is "just fine." However, I have discovered that therapy has been one of the most effective and helpful tools in my arsenal to become healthier. I didn't know how depressed and *loud* my internal debates and self-condemnations were until I went through therapy. It amazes me to consider how differently and how much better I feel now, like a literal weight has lifted from my body and a gloomy fog from my mind. I could not have imagined that I could feel better than I did prior to therapy. My former state had become my normal.

Therapists are educated and trained to help with mental and emotional issues, especially trauma, that other people (read: pastors and spiritual leaders) are simply not equipped to help with. By all means, find a Christian therapist, which was what I did. I was able to find a great therapist on www.psychologytoday.com. I was even able to filter for someone who was not only Christian but who also took insurance.

One of the methods my therapist utilizes is called Internal Family Systems (IFS). It was originally established by Richard Schwartz and continues to demonstrate effectiveness in clinical studies. I have found it to be incredibly powerful in creating healthy shifts in my mind, taking the process I outlined above to reframe my false narratives many steps further. I learned how those false narratives are stored in my body and retriggered by tension in certain muscles, as well as how to address and care for my inner child—the one who grips so tightly to these false narratives as a means of self-protection. In some ways, it reminds me of inner healing prayer. On the IFS website, www.ifs-institute.com, you can also find therapists and practitioners who are certified in practicing IFS in your area.

During one session, my therapist led me through a process that helped regulate my emotions, one that I could also practice on my own:

1. Breathe: bring awareness of self through breath.

2. Notice pacing and adjust to appropriate tempo for the situation.

3. Positive self-talk: speak truth/reality statements to automatic negative thoughts, or ANTs, as she called them.

4. Recognize boundaries: what I can control vs. the other person's control.

5. Pinpoint what is causing that feeling.

Learning to regulate your emotions is important in growing in freedom because often, as adults, our anxiety, discouragement, fear, and so on come from unresolved emotional needs as children. We might know mentally that we are loved and secure adults, but our bodies under stress can immediately transport us back to a time when we believed otherwise.

You can certainly grow in developing awareness of false narratives on your own, but working with a therapist has accelerated that growth for me. I'm introspective by nature, but internal work that would have taken me years—invisible walls in my mind that wouldn't yield—turned into breakthroughs. Not to mention how much less tiring it is to have someone help me with the process rather than carrying the load alone. It is still hard work, but it's also refreshing to have someone you can lean on 100 percent without worrying about overburdening them—someone whose *job* it is to be there for you.

Finally, be sure to find a therapist who is a good fit for you. Sometimes a therapist's style or personality may simply not work with what you need, and that's okay. You are the one paying for this service, and it is for your benefit, not the therapist's. If a therapist doesn't seem like the right fit, don't be afraid to move on and try someone else.

BOOKS

To learn more about family systems therapy:

The Family Crucible by Augustus Y. Napier and Carl A. Whitaker

Ties that Stress: The New Family Imbalance by David Elkind

Generation to Generation: Family Process in Church and Synagogue by Edwin H. Friedman

Books by Dr. David Augsburger:

Pastoral Counseling across Cultures

Conflict Mediation across Cultures: Pathways and Patterns

Caring Enough to Confront: How to Understand and Express Your Deepest Feelings toward Others

Here are some books that have been helpful in my journey to better emotional regulation, a solid self, and deeper connection with God:

Calmer, Easier, Happier Parenting by Noël Janis-Norton

The Highly Sensitive Person by Elaine Aron

Switch On Your Brain by Caroline Leaf

Self-Therapy: A Step-by-Step Guide to Creating Wholeness and Healing Your Inner Child Using IFS, a New, Cutting-Edge Psychotherapy by Jay Earley

Desiring the Kingdom by James K. A. Smith

Emotionally Healthy Spirituality by Peter Scazzero

Emotionally Healthy Leadership by Peter Scazzero

Life of the Beloved: Spiritual Living in a Secular World by Henri Nouwen

The Wounded Healer: Ministry in Contemporary Society by Henri Nouwen

My Utmost for His Highest by Oswald Chambers

SPIRITUAL DISCIPLINES

Since there are many books and resources available concerning spiritual disciplines, I will keep this simple. I think the most important aspects of any spiritual discipline are consistency and finding whatever helps you to engage and connect with God the most. Never forget that the objective of spiritual disciplines is not to prove you are a good Christian, but simply to connect with God and to align your mind and heart with God's. Being consistent yet flexible can help avoid becoming overly legalistic about your spiritual disciplines.

Yes, sometimes doing the same thing every day can feel routinized and stale over time, but I commit to doing it anyway and have never regretted it. It's the small, incremental growth that at first might be unseen that will make for lasting, *enduring* transformation. Sometimes, I do change it up and do something different if I sense myself lapsing into a legalistic posture. For instance, I might sing a few worship songs that are particularly relevant to what I might be going through instead of going through my prayer list line by line as I normally would. I find changing things up temporarily brings a new appreciation for my regular disciplines when I return to them.

Furthermore, don't underestimate intentionality and mindset when approaching any spiritual discipline. I'd definitely recommend quality over quantity. Trust that God *wants* to meet with you. God is present because God has promised this is so, not because you feel God or because you've been a "good boy" or "good girl." God has also given us the Holy Spirit as a guarantee of this promise. Five minutes of intentional, purposeful focus and acknowledgement of God's presence can deepen your connection and make space for God to move within you—maybe more so than an hour of going through the motions just to say you did it. (Although I also believe this can bear fruit too because God is gracious! Basically, any move we make toward God will invite God to reciprocate.)

Here are the spiritual disciplines I have found valuable:

Scripture

There are many different ways to interact with Scripture. I grew up reading the Bible from cover to cover a few chapters a day. I also reflected on small sections at a time, writing down what I observed, my interpretation of what I observed, and finally, how to apply that interpretation to my life.

For example, an actual excerpt from my high school journal:

August 9, 1999
Passage: Romans 4:1–8
Observation:

- *Abraham believed in God, and it was credited to him as righteousness, not because of his works*
- *A man is credited as righteous because of his faith, not work*
- *David says blessed are those whose sins are forgiven*

Interpretation:

- *Abraham did sin, but because he trusted God, he was said to be righteous*
- *If you want to be righteous, you have to have faith in God*
- *Blessed are those who believe that God wipes away our sins and gives us salvation*

Application:

- *Trust in God to be righteous—from my faith, good works will come . . .*
- *After I repent for a sin, I need to trust that God has forgiven me and wiped me clean, so I shouldn't feel guilty*

Nothing too revelatory. But this practice established a strong foundation for naturally interacting with Scripture as more than just a written text. I learned to incorporate it into my life and my being.

Nowadays, I still read a couple chapters of the Bible every day and read from a devotional book occasionally. Though I don't always journal, I always reflect on how what I am reading connects to my life. I always ask God, "Let your word speak to me," before I open the word or the devotional.

Another way of engaging with God's word I learned about in seminary is called *lectio divina*. It is a way of reading Scripture that is rooted in monasticism. Basically, it entails reading the same passage of Scripture several times. Each time the passage is read, there is a given focus. The reading is followed by a period of silence and then a period where people share in relation to the given focus. In the most recent Bible-study group I led, we read through the Gospel of John passage by passage using *lectio divina*. The first time the passage was read, we focused on any word or phrase that stood out to us. The second time, we focused on what God might be saying to us personally. The third and last time, we focused on what God might be saying to us as a community. Before we began, we assigned three different readers to minimize disruptions in the process. The practice of being silent and listening to God's word in community was powerful, and insights that came forth were beautiful as people shared how God spoke to them. And perhaps more powerful and beautiful was the sensation of taking time out of the busyness and chaos of life to meander and dwell in God's presence together. Being silent on one's own is one thing, but being intentionally silent to listen to God corporately seemed to magnify the experience.

The reason I like *lectio divina* so much is because it reminds me that God is the one who moves and initiates. In other words, I don't have to try so hard. The *way* I study Scripture can actually communicate and reinforce what I believe about God. I'm not rejecting proper exegesis (I am a seminary grad, after all), but *lectio divina* provided a balance to a highly intellectualized approach to Scripture that had always been a part of my Christian experience. It reminds me that God is a God in whom I can rest.

Prayer

I learned as a child to structure prayer according to the acronym "ACTS," and I have a prayer list that I go through daily, still following this guide as an adult. If it works, why change it?

> A: Adoration (praises to God)
> C: Confession of sins
> T: Thanksgiving
> S: Supplication (requests)

The one thing I have changed in my prayer life, however, is adding time with God in silence. Every day, once I have gone through my prayer list, I sit with God quietly, asking if there is anything God would like to say to me. I then sit silently, and after a time, I may gently respond if I sense God saying something.

Sometimes, it helps to imagine myself sitting at a café with Jesus, enjoying our favorite warm beverages. I imagine this scenario because this is one of my favorite ways of connecting with my most intimate friends. Other times, I imagine us on a beach, as the ocean has always vividly reminded me of God's presence. Sometimes, after waiting in silence, nothing comes, or Jesus just smiles at me! In that case, I simply enjoy that God is present with me. In that moment, I remember that I am not merely a workhorse but that God desires communion with me.

Other times, when I am in a difficult season—when I'm feeling tired or overwhelmed and it's hard to pray—I forego going through my prayer list and simply sit with God in silence. Silence creates space. We tend to fill our lives with noise and things, but quietness within is an essential element to tuning our hearts and ears to the Holy Spirit. When we are silent, space is created that God is able to fill.

Lately, I have also incorporated breathing prayers based on Scripture throughout my day, like when I'm driving, grocery shopping, or cutting tile (I've been working on the floor in our house). When I encounter anxiety, I have found this confession particularly helpful in quieting myself within and aligning myself with God: "All that I am and all that I have are yours." If this interests you, you might find *Breath Prayer Guides* by Bill Gaultiere helpful. It can be found at www.soulshepherding.org.

Sabbath

I heard Peter Scazzero, the author of *Emotionally Healthy Spirituality*, speak at a conference. He summed up perfectly why Sabbath matters: "Sabbath teaches us that God still loves us even when we're not productive." Rest is an important spiritual discipline, yet many of us feel like we need someone's permission to rest. It's hard to rest when it seems like the world never turns off and is always demanding something.

This discipline is probably the most challenging for me. Scazzero encourages a designated day each week to take as one's Sabbath, and I can't say that I follow this. Even though I feel like I have been on one long sabbatical (that I initially accepted grudgingly), I have had to learn to rest within that. Currently, I play volleyball once a week with a group of people who not only love playing as much as I do but who have also become a true community for me. I used to feel apologetic and guilty that I spent so much time doing something that was "unproductive" and that wasn't meaningful "spiritually." Thoughts like, "I should be at home preparing dinner, cleaning the house, or finishing my book" plagued me. But then I realized that God *wanted* this for me and that this *was* meaningful spiritually. God delighted in me doing something that was 100 percent pure fun and joy for me. Now I rarely let anything interrupt this routine because it is so refreshing for me. While playing volleyball is not strictly restful physically, it does rest my soul in a different way.

However, physical rest is also important, and I am learning to fold rhythms of physical rest into my life more consistently. For instance, I often forget to eat when I'm working on something. But I realized that my consuming drive to finish projects originated from a spiral of anxiety as I wondered whether the finished result would be good enough. I also depended on adrenaline to get things done, a practice solidified from years of racing to meet deadlines in school. I've had to learn to take breaks (and that breaks are good), eat regular meals no matter where I am in a project, and put down whatever I'm working on to sleep at a reasonable hour. I have definitely made errors due to fatigue and overstrain because I didn't take breaks, which ultimately made not taking breaks counterproductive. Breaks and sufficient sleep give me renewed energy for my work and clearer perspective.

Furthermore, as an introvert, I absolutely need rest from social engagements. I am intentional about not scheduling too many social events or meetings, usually limiting them to one or two per week. I also like to keep at least one Saturday per month free of any social plans. If I begin feeling overextended, I will give myself an entire week without social engagements and draw back on activities like texting.

Again, breaks are good. I can sense when I truly need a day to slow down. I know the activities that help me feel rested when I've been pushing myself too hard: spending a day unplugged from electronics, reading a book, journaling, picking up food instead of cooking, and even lying down in a dark closet to eliminate all stimulation. The reality is that most people are more likely to ask for more than to insist you rest. You must give *yourself* permission to rest—and really, you already have the highest permission from God. You are more than what you accomplish, how much money you make, how many projects you can finish, how much status you garner, or how many parties you are invited to. Rest is good and is not simply for the lazy. It is a witness to the world that your value comes from God and not productivity—that lasting fruitfulness comes from be-ing *with* God, not striving for it.

Ultimately, when it comes to our spiritual disciplines and worship, I think we simply need more stillness and more silence.

CPSIA information can be obtained
at www.ICGtesting.com
Printed in the USA
FSHW022304271021